ETHNIC CHRONOLOGY SERIES
NUMBER 17

The Estonians in America 1627-1975

A Chronology & Fact Book

Compiled and edited by

Jaan Pennar

in Association with

Tönu Parming
and
P. Peter Rebane

1975
OCEANA PUBLICATIONS, INC
DOBBS FERRY, NEW YORK

Library of Congress Cataloging in Publication Data

Pennar, Jaan.
    The Estonians in America, 1627-1975.

    (Ethnic chronology series ; no. 17)
    "Documents": p.
    Bibliography: p.
    Includes index.
    1. Estonian Americans--History--Chronology.
2. Estonian Americans--History--Sources.
I. Parming, Tönu, joint author. II. Rebane, P.
Peter, joint author. III. Title. IV. Series.
E184.E7P46   973'.04'94545   75-9799
ISBN 0-379-00519-0

Manufactured in the United States of America.

TABLE OF CONTENTS

PREFACE

The Estonian Learned Society in America is pleased to have sponsored the research for the present study. Since the history of the Estonians in America is of rather recent vintage -- mostly a saga of the past seventy-five years -- the presentation of a definitive work is hardly possible. The society, however, hopes that the present pioneering volume, although a chronology and fact book rather than an analysis, will stimulate further study of the group's history in this country, both by Estonian and non-Estonian scholars.

On behalf of the society I would like to express our gratitude to the committee responsible for the research and preparation of the manuscript: Jaan Pennar, Research Associate, Center for Education in Industrial Nations, Teachers College, Columbia University, who headed the committee and was the principal researcher and compiler; Tõnu Parming, Assistant Professor of Sociology at the University of Maryland, College Park, who as secretary of the society administratively co-ordinated the project; and P. Peter Rebane, Assistant Professor of History at Pennsylvania State University, Ogontz Campus. Professors Parming and Rebane contributed substantially to the final version of the volume, and the former supplied a significant number of the chronology entries.

Special thanks are also due to the following society members for their valuable assistance: Eve Simson, Assistant Professor of Sociology at Indiana State University, South Bend, for translating source materials from Estonian to English; Hilja Kukk, Reference Librarian, Hoover Institution, Stanford, California, for procuring source materials on Estonians in northern California and Alaska during the Russian period; and Marju Rink Parming, Reference Librarian at the United States General Accounting Office Library, Washington, D.C., for editing and proofreading the manuscript. Lastly, the society acknowledges with gratitude the financial support of the following three Estonian academic organizations, which made possible the research on which the book is based: Eesti Korporatsioonide Liit, Eesti Üliõpilaste Selts, and Korporatsioon Filiae Patriae. Dr. Pennar also received a personal award from the Estonian American National Council.

Viktor Kõressaar
President
Estonian Learned Society
in America

New York City
February 24, 1975

INTRODUCTION

Estonians are known to have lived in America in early colonial times. They were not many then -- the present study documents only two, a drummer and a saddlemaker. In the seventeenth century Estonia was part of the Swedish realm and Sweden encouraged settlement in the New World, which accounts for the presence of the two Estonians -- and perhaps others whose traces have disappeared.

The Great Northern War (1700-1721) ended Swedish rule in Estonia. Now under Tsarist Russian rule, Estonians left no new record of a presence in America until the nineteenth century. The majority of the early immigrants during this next period of Estonian-American history were sailors in the Tsarist navy or ordinary seamen who jumped ship in American ports. Some Estonians might have come here when Russia held sway over northern California and Alaska, but proof is lacking. There were some among the early immigrants who preferred life in America to service in the Russian army and fled their homeland because of this. Although there are stories of Estonians participating in the California Gold Rush of 1848, the first Estonian immigrant whose presence in nineteenth century America can be definitely proven arrived in 1855.

The size of the Estonian immigration in these earlier times is not known, since no records were kept by American immigration authorities on Estonians until 1922. The reason for this was that Estonia was part of Russia, and Estonians arriving here were consequently classified as "Russians." However, official American governmental estimates made in 1924 placed the number of residents of Estonian ancestry at 5,100 in 1890; 44,900 in 1910; and 69,200 in 1920. An American expert on immigration writing at the same time placed the figure for 1920 at an even higher 200,000. There is no way of verifying these estimates. If the largest of them is used, then there are now about 400,000 Americans of at least partial Estonian ancestry.

For the purposes of the present book, the term "Estonian" includes anyone whose ancestry can be traced back to the territorial area known as Estonia, located on the shores of the northeastern corner of the Baltic Sea in Europe. Thus, Germans, Russians and Jews from Estonia are considered to be "Estonians" along with the ethnic Estonians, who made up about 88% of the population of Estonia in 1934.

The materials in the present volume are organized to reflect the characteristics of three distinct phases of Estonian-American history: the period up to 1922; the years from 1922 through 1945; and the period since

then. Patterns of settlement, the organization of the
ethnic community, special achievements and events, and
political activities are covered within each period.
The documents section supports the major points brought
forth in the chronology.

Setting aside the colonial times, we now turn to the
first Estonian immigrants of the nineteenth century, who
have already been characterized as ship-jumping seamen.
As the century wore on, however, many different types of
immigrants appear. Some were individual professional
men, but a much larger number were rural settlers. Many
Estonian farmers and their families came from the Crimea
and other parts of Russia, where they had settled earlier. At the turn of the century a number of Estonian
villages were established in Wisconsin and the Dakotas.
Later, settlements appeared in the Rocky Mountain states
and the Pacific Northwest. There were Estonian fishermen in Oregon even before the arrival of the farmers.
In 1897 the first Estonian-language newspaper in the
United States was published in New York by an enterprising clergyman. The Estonian Lutheran congregation
founded in New York the following year still exists
today.

The 1905 Revolution in Russia brought the first wave
of Estonian political emigres to America's shores. They
came in large numbers and settled in the cities. Almost
all of them appear to have been socialist-oriented, and
in 1909 they founded their own newspaper, Uus Ilm (The
New World), which still appears today. It was not unusual for Estonians at the time to adopt socialist ideas.
In their own country the economic, social and cultural
upper class was German, while the political rulers were
Russian. Most, though not all, Estonian political leaders of the period espoused some type of socialist or
Marxist ideals. Estonians in the New World pretty much
followed this pattern.

The 1917 October Revolution in Russia and Estonia's
declaration of independence in 1918 had a profound impact on the Estonian-American community. Some returned
to their native land. Among those who stayed, a division
developed over political issues and ideology. A majority,
including many of socialist persuasion, began to lobby
on behalf of the new Republic of Estonia. However,
others moved further to the left, and some joined the
American Communist Party.

The period from 1922 to 1945 was one of retrenchment.
Although both the Bureau of the Census and the Immigration and Naturalization Service made "Estonia" a classi-
ficatory category, immigration from Estonia was a mere
3,100 for the whole period. A number of the immigrants
even returned to Estonia. In the 1920s the Estonian-
American community attempted to establish a unified and
politically neutral centralized organization, but with-

out success. Consequently, during the late 1920s and
early 1930s a veritable scramble developed, as rival
communist and nationalist-oriented groups formed clubs
and societies all over the United States, competing for
new members. It is in this period that the now pres-
tigious New York Estonian Educational Society was founded. In 1931 the society sponsored an Estonian-language
monthly, <u>Meie Tee</u> (Our Path), which still appears regularly today.

Towards the close of the period under consideration,
during World War II, Estonian-American community leaders
and the Estonian Consulate General in New York fought
hard to insure that the United States would not accord
legal recognition to the Soviet annexation of Estonia
in 1940. Their sentiments were fully supported by the
American press, which reported on events in Estonia.
The American government itself had taken a strong stand
on the issue and to this day legally recognizes the
Republic of Estonia.

The period from 1945 to the present saw the arrival
of a new wave of Estonian political exiles in the United
States, numbering about 14,000. To be sure, not all of
them were politically motivated in leaving Estonia, but
the wide majority was. They were truly "displaced persons" because of the political and ideological changes
which World War II had brought about in Europe. Unlike
the Estonian socialist exiles of 1905, they wanted nothing to do with Marxist ideas. They had suffered
through a brutal year of Soviet rule in 1940-1941 and
three years of German occupation afterwards. Rather
than live under Stalinist repression, over 100,000
Estonian citizens fled westward (about 9% of the prewar
population). At the end of the war they chose permanent
exile rather than return to Soviet-ruled Estonia. When
the opportunity arose, many opted for resettlement in
the United States. Staunchly anticommunist, the new
immigrants further isolated many in the earlier wave of
Estonian political exiles from mainstream Estonian-
American society.

The postwar emigres began arriving in America in
1945, the first groups crossing the Atlantic in 30 to
40-foot sailboats. These "Viking boat" Estonians came
from Sweden, fearing that the Swedish government might
forcibly repatriate Estonian refugees there to the Soviet Union. A total of fifteen such boats arrived in
the United States before the 1948 Displaced Persons Act
opened the country for resettlement to thousands of
Estonians in European refugee camps.

A major difference between the "old" and the "new"
Estonian-Americans, other than in their attitudes toward
communism, was the latter's well-developed ethnic self-
awareness and high degree of political consciousness.
Also, the newcomers were eager to resume "normal lives",

having suffered through five years of war and five years of life in refugee camps. They found little, if any, prejudice against Estonians in this country, and most of their major cultural values fit in well with those in America. Thus, the group quickly attained a middle-class status. The educational level of the younger segment is extremely high -- a college education and beyond is typical. As such, the group's members have made significant individual contributions to American culture, science and academic life. Meanwhile, they have continued to make significant contributions to Estonian culture and scholarship in exile. Estonian-Americans have an extensive organizational network which both perpetuates their culture and identity and provides for the waging of a political struggle on an international scale to free Estonia of Soviet rule. The approximately 20,000 first and second-generation Estonians in America have over 300 organizations, or, roughly, one organization for every 65 people.

Since there are exceedingly few published sources on Estonians in America, and since the group's archives are in the initial stages of organization at present, it is quite likely that a few important events and activities have escaped the compilers' attention. Hopefully, future researchers will fill the gaps and expand on the materials presented herein.

THE "OLD IMMIGRANTS":   THE PERIOD UNTIL 1922

THE COLONIAL PERIOD

1627   There is no trace of the "Estonians and Livo-
              nians" who left their homeland in 1627 to set-
              tle at the mouth of the Delaware River, re-
              ports an Estonian chronicler. At the time,
              Estonia was part of the Swedish realm, and
              settlement in the Swedish colony in the Dela-
              ware River area was officially encouraged.
              Because Estonian names at the time blended
              easily with those of the Swedes, Finns and
              Dutch in the colony, it is difficult to prove
              an Estonian presence.

1654   Proof of an Estonian presence in the settle-
              ment of New Sweden on the Delaware River is
              provided by the list of officers and men in
              the colony. One of them, Johan Schalbrick, a
              drummer, was described as hailing from Reval,
              the German name for the capital of Estonia,
              Tallinn.

1657   Another Estonian, "born at Reval [Tallinn] on
              the Gulf of Finland in 1625" Martin(us) Hoff-
              man, arrived in New Amsterdam [New York]. A
              restless young man who claimed his father was
              an officer in the Swedish cavalry, Hoffman
              started to work as a saddlemaker but soon took
              off up the Hudson River to fight the Indians.
              Subsequently, he acquired a small vessel with
              which he plied the river between Albany and
              New Amsterdam. He was given a large tract of
              land in Ulster County for his service to the
              Crown and acquired additional land in neigh-
              boring Dutchess County across the Hudson. In
              1664 Hoffman married Emmerentje de With [De
              Witt] who bore him five children. His great-
              granddaughter, Cornelia Hoffman (born 1734),
              married Isaac Roosevelt, which makes her the
              great-great-great-grandmother of Franklin
              Delano Roosevelt, the thirty-second president
              of the United States.

18th   Estonia became a province of Russia as a re-
Century   sult of Sweden's defeat in the Great Northern
              War (1700-1721). Population losses were se-
              vere, the country was ravaged and recovery
              was slow. There is no evidence of any Esto-
              nians emigrating to the New World during the
              eighteenth century, although a few might have
              done so.

THE NINETEENTH CENTURY

Early
19th
Century

Alaska, which was then under Russian rule, was extensively explored and charted by Imperial Russian naval and scientific explorers, among whom there is a number of Estonians. These include Admiral Adam von Krusenstern, Count Otto von Kotzebue, Dr. Karl Espenberg, Dr. Peter H. Aliman, Dr. Johan Friedrich Escholtz, Dr. H. Sieval and F.E. Lenz, a physicist. Most of the listed doctors also worked as botanists, zoologists, meteorologists, cartographers, and even geologists.

It took two to three years to sail from St. Petersburg [now Leningrad], then the capital of Russia, to Alaska and back around the world. Three major expeditions have been recorded: 1803-1806, 1815-1818, and 1823-1826. The first expedition was led by Krusenstern and the last two by Kotzebue. There are sounds, capes, and settlements in Alaska named after Krusenstern, Espenberg and Kotzebue.

Mid-19th
Century

Estonian sailors, serving on Russian vessels, jumped ship on several occasions during the nineteenth century, both on the East and West Coasts. Some of the more adventurous among them are reputed to have participated in the California Gold Rush of 1848, but definite proof is lacking. It is a fact, however, that one Jaan Sepp arrived in New York in 1855 as a seaman. After a stint as a stevedore and construction worker, he left for the West Coast where under the name of John Smith he became a trapper and a barger. Having made enough money, he decided to return to Estonia, which he did, but not before losing the $2,000 he had saved gambling aboard the ship taking him back to Europe.

Other Estonians could have been in the United States at the time. For example, Polk's San Francisco Directory for 1861 records such popular Estonian family names as Luts, Kull, and Ott, but there is no firm proof that the bearers of these names were necessarily Estonians. Among the first known Estonian settlers in nineteenth century America were Fred Bekmann and Mike Anderson [Mihkel Sau]. They arrived in 1871 and 1872, respectively, and both went to Oregon. They were preceded in the country, however, by Professor Hermann Eduard von Holst (see page 3).

1887   Thomas Ackman from Pärnu, Estonia, opened a
              bar and hostel in San Francisco, which became
              the meeting place for Estonian seamen and new
              immigrants.

1892   Hermann Eduard von Holst became the first
              chairman of the newly created Department of
              History at the University of Chicago. Holst,
              born in Estonia, immigrated to the United
              States in 1867. Having studied at the Univer-
              sity of Dorpat [now Tartu] in Estonia, he re-
              ceived a doctoral degree in history from the
              University of Heidelberg in Germany. Holst
              authored a number of important works on Amer-
              ican history, among which are the multi-vol-
              ume The Constitutional and Political History
              of the United States (1873), and a biography
              entitled John C. Calhoun (1882). In 1894 he
              wrote the important two-volume The French Re-
              volution Tested by Mirabeau's Career. Holst
              also was a professor at the Universities of
              Strasbourg (France) and Freiburg (Germany).
              In 1872 he had married Annie Isabelle Hart,
              of an old New England family. Holst died in
              Freiburg, Germany.

              December. Johann Jurgens, who had arrived
              from Estonia a decade earlier, died in Chica-
              go during Christmas. Jurgens, whose knowledge
              of English was excellent, wrote a number of
              brochures and pamphlets for the Salvation Army,
              in which he held the rank of captain.

1894   A group of Estonians settled near Fort Pierre,
              South Dakota. They came here by way of the
              Crimea in Russia, where they had settled ear-
              lier. Their leader, John Moor [Johan Määr]
              wrote, "We are now 7 families (36 souls) who
              have settled here. We make a living from many
              things, primarily cattle breeding... I don't
              know much about Estonians in America but I do
              know that other Estonians have settled here.
              The places where one can also find Estonians
              are San Francisco, California, and Oregon, on
              the West Coast, by the Pacific Ocean. There
              are also some Estonians in New York who are
              mostly handicraftsmen. On the Pacific Coast
              there are some fishermen and seamen who are
              still foot-loose...."

1896   January. The Reverend Hans Rebane arrived in
              New York at the invitation of the German Mis-
              souri Lutheran Synod to become the pastor to

Estonians and Latvians of Lutheran faith in
the United States. His first efforts to establish contact with his flock in the major
eastern cities from Baltimore to Boston yiel-
ded very few Estonians but a larger number of
Latvians. Rebane reported that most of the
Estonians whom he found scattered in the area
held low-paying domestic or factory jobs, except for one J. Gutman, who was a trolley operator in Brooklyn and therefore earned a good
salary. (See Document No. 1.)

1897   March. Rev. Rebane launched the first Estonian-language newspaper in the United States,
the bi-monthly Eesti Amerika Postimees (Estonian American Courier). The paper appeared
fairly regularly until Rebane's sudden death
in 1911. About half of each issue was devoted to religious topics and the remainder to
news about Estonians in North America and immigration matters of interest to Estonians at
home. Occasionally there were editorial opin-
ions expressed on a variety of subjects, including the evils of alcohol, which was one of
the pastor's major complaints. Another matter
which seemingly concerned him was the godless-
ness of the Estonian socialists who flocked
to America after the 1905 Revolution in Russia.
The newspaper's editorial offices were in the
German Lutheran Pilgrimage House at 8 State
Street in New York City. The first issue of
the paper also announced the first Estonian-
language church service to be held in the
country, at the German St. Matthew Church in
New York City. It was attended by 15 people.

Summer. The first Estonian Lutheran congregation in America was established at the Estonian settlement in South Dakota (see page
3). A second congregation was founded in
New York City on February 20, 1898. The latter quickly became the largest Estonian Lutheran congregation in the country and still
exists today.

1898   The Eesti Amerika Postimees received the following news from a "kinsman" in San Francisco,
M. Oiderman: "There are more than 100 Estonians living here, and about as many Latvian
folks... There is a lot of excitement here,
too, about the Alaskan gold... Even from our
Estonian community there are 14 young men who
left here for the Alaskan gold fields... It

is fun to live in America but it sometimes
saddens one not to hear the melodious singing of Estonian maidens. Among the large
number of Estonians who live here there are
only three Estonian womenfolk."

The first Estonian-language book printed in
the United States, Juhan Sepp's Dollarite
maalt (From the Land of Dollars), was published by Mike Anderson at 103 Suomi Avenue,
Astoria, Oregon. The same year E. Melldorf
published in New York, at his own expense, a
work entitled Lühike Ingliskeeleõpetus ja
Sõnaraamat (A Short Course in English and a
Dictionary), which sold for sixty cents a
copy.

Estonian-born George Alexius placed a wreath
on the funnel of the sunken American battle-
ship Maine in Havana harbor. Alexius took
part in the Spanish-American War, serving on
the Brooklyn, and he received a number of
medals and decorations. He served in the U.S.
Navy until 1907, when he was placed in charge
of lighthouses in California. He ended up at
the Cape Scotch Lighthouse on Unimak Island
in Alaska. Service was considered so rough
there, that after every two years one was giv-
en a year's vacation. Provisions were delivered once a year and mail three times. The
mail, however, had to be fished out of the
water. After forty years of service, Alexius
retired and settled in Los Angeles, where he
participated in the life of the local Estonian community. He died at the age of 85 in
1961.

May. The first Estonian social organization
in the United States was founded in New York,
the Amerika Eesti Heategev Selts (American
Estonian Beneficial Society). E. Melldorf
was elected president; Alex Rebane, vice president; M. Pai, secretary; R. Sarlandt, assistant secretary; and M. Bernstein, auditor.

October. Juhan Sepp wrote in Amerika Eesti
Postimees that if in the future someone were
to compile a history of Estonian-Americans,
he should not overlook the Estonians of Astoria, Oregon. Sepp claimed that Astoria,
located at the mouth of the Columbia River,
was the headquarters for Estonians on the
whole Pacific Coast. They had been there

for 30 years, and one of the earliest settlers
was one Georg Smith. Sepp personally knew
two Estonian fishermen who had been there for
20 years. Fishing was the mainstay of the
local economy. There were also a large number of Finns in Astoria with whom the Estonians closely associated, to the extent that
some Estonians switched to Finnish as their
everyday language. This was not too difficult, since the languages are closely related. An estimated 25 Estonians were residents of Astoria at the time of Sepp's article.

THE EARLY TWENTIETH CENTURY

1900   Spring. Gustav Sommi and his family arrived
in Bloomville in Lincoln County, Wisconsin,
from Samara, Russia, where they had settled
from Estonia earlier. By 1911 the number of
Estonians in Lincoln and neighboring Langlade
Counties had grown to 82. An Estonian-named
village, Irma, was established ten miles from
the railroad stop at Gleason. The latter also became an Estonian village. The Estonian
immigrants were guided to Wisconsin by two
Estonian pastors in this country, first by
Reverend Hans Rebane, and after his death,
by Reverend Conrad Klemmer. Both were in
touch with the company selling land to settlers in the area, the Wisconsin Valley Land
Company. The first Estonian Lutheran church
in America was built in Gleason in 1914. Although the Estonian communities in Irma and
Gleason have lost most of their offspring
through assimilation or by their movement to
cities, the church still functions during occasional midwestern Estonian get-togethers.
However, a few Estonian families are left
there, the wealthiest being the brothers Johannes and Karl Pay [Pai], who own about 460
acres of farmland and who arrived in this
country, with their parents, from Estonia in
1907. The grandson of the founder of the
settlement, Alfred Sommi, was the leading or-
ganizer of an Estonian exhibit in New York in
1929.

Estonian immigrants at the turn of the century were, by and large, taken for Russians,
since their country was part of the Tsarist
Empire, and most arrived in America with

Russian passports or papers. An interesting
story related to such a mistaken identity
occurred in China during the Boxer Rebellion,
in which both American and Russian military
units participated. After the fighting, the
American and Russian units established contact to talk things over, but this was difficult because of the lack of a common language. The Americans announced that there
was a Russian in their unit who could be used
as an interpreter. But when this "Russian"
faced the real Russians, he found it difficult to translate. He turned out to be an
Estonian who had entered the United States on
a Russian passport. A solution was found,
nevertheless. The Russian unit also produced
an Estonian serving in its ranks. The two
Estonians communicated perfectly and inter-
preted the conversation of the two commanders
in their respective languages by way of the
Estonian.

1902   The first Estonian settlers arrived from Tver
and Saratov in Russia to farm land near Dick-
enson, North Dakota. They were later joined
by others from the Crimea. The settlement
was called "New England." In the 1930s there
were still 20 Estonians in the settlement, on
farms ranging from 300 to 1,000 acres in size.
Many "New England" Estonians had left by then
for the neighboring towns to become small
businessmen. They intermarried and became
increasingly assimilated.

October. An Estonian Lutheran congregation
was established in Philadelphia with Mihkel
Õunapuu as its lay leader. There were 16
members in the congregation. The largest Estonian congregation in the United States at
the time, with 150 members, was in New York.

1904   The first Estonian social organization in
San Francisco, the Eestlaste Laulu Selts
(Estonians Singing Society), was established.
It soon changed its name to Vastastikku Abi-
andmise Selts (Mutual Assistance Society),
which organized the first Estonian social
event on the West Coast that was open to the
public. The leading figure in these activities was Rudolf Sarlandt. The San Francisco
earthquake of 1906 dispersed the society's
members, including the treasurer, who disappeared with $200.

Spring. Estonians from Portland, Oregon, established a settlement 90 miles south of that
city at Rose Lodge. In the mid-1930s there
were still 11 Estonian farms in the settlement.

1905   Ivan Narodny [Jaan Sibul] arrived in New York
together with Maxim Gorki's adopted son,
Zinovy Peshkov. On his arrival Narodny
claimed he was John D. Rockefeller, and he
produced a false Russian passport in that
name. His stated purpose was to collect ten
million dollars for a revolution in Russia.
He was immediately welcomed at the American
Revolutionary Club on Fifth Avenue, one of
whose members was Mark Twain. Narodny soon
was selling twenty-five dollar shares in an
organization dedicated to toppling the Tsarist regime in Russia. In 1918, when Estonia
fought for its independence, Narodny switched
his support to that cause. Later he became
an art dealer and critic. In 1908 Narodny
had married a soprano and concert artist, Ma-
rie Mieler, who also was Estonian born. Narodny died in 1953 at the age of 79 at his
home in Sharon, Connecticut.

October. A second Estonian social organization, Lootus (Hope), was established in New
York, to compete with the older American
Estonian Beneficial Society. The two organizations merged in January, 1910, to become
the New York Estonian Society. Among those
active in the latter were Hans Pymson, John
Metsalo and John Paist.

1906   The 1905 Revolution in Tsarist Russia caused
the first wave of Estonian political exiles
to seek refuge in the United States. The exiles were all socialists fleeing the Tsarist
police. The Socialist Party of America created a special Estonian Department in 1906.
However, it was shortly turned into an independent Estonian Social-Democratic Association. Among the more active Estonian socialists at the time was Hans Pöögelmann, who
became involved not only in politics but also in the arts. He was the moving force behind the Estonian Professional Art Theatre
in New York, which was also established in
1906. Pöögelmann subsequently became editor
(1911-1917) of the Estonian socialist newspaper Uus Ilm (The New World) in New York.

He returned to Estonia in 1918 and then went
to Soviet Russia, where he eventually became
a high official in the Communist International (Comintern). Pöögelmann perished in the
Stalinist purges of 1938.

A settlement called "Estonia" was established
in northwest Wisconsin, near the city of Hay-
ward. This was the beginning of a scheme to
settle large numbers of Estonians onto a wide
tract of land that had been cleared by a lumber company. The future president of independent Estonia, Konstantin Päts, personally
came to look over the land in July and August.
Päts was, at the time, a political activist
and newspaper publisher with considerable
influence in Tsarist-ruled Estonia. He lived
in exile in Finland, however, because of the
events of the 1905 Revolution. Päts came to
the United States at the expense of the firm
which sought to settle Estonians on the land
and was shown a model farm. Since it made a
good impression upon him, Päts let it be
known that he favored the creation of a large
Estonian settlement on the tract. In the
meantime, however, an Estonian-American, J.
Sarei, personally had investigated the tract,
talking to a few Estonian settlers there whom
Päts had not seen. He found that working
conditions were harsh. Three and four-foot
tree stumps had to be cleared, and living
conditions were most primitive, with two
children in one family having died during the
winter. When these facts became known to
Päts, he sent a friend to doublecheck them
and soon reversed his recommendation. Estonians who had already settled there gave up
in a year and went on to other parts of the
country. The idea of creating a large Estonian (and, possibly, socialist) farming colony in northwest Wisconsin thus never bore
fruit.
        The germ of the idea probably originated
with merchant marine Captain Keyl, who
brought Päts over, and whose brother, the
Reverend Keyl, was in charge of the German
Lutheran Pilgrimage House in New York, which
served as the headquarters of the first Estonian pastor in this country. Captain Keyl
had apparently invested in the settlement
scheme, and those who had already arrived
there before Päts came to inspect the site
paid from five to fifteen dollars per acre,

for which they obtained long-term loans. The
settlers could also work in a neighboring
lumber mill for nine dollars a week, with
room and board costing four dollars a week.
Two horses, for the sake of reference, cost
three hundred dollars and a cow about thirty-
five dollars.

1907   Twenty-year old Alex Semlek arrived from Tallinn, hoping to become a tailor in Philadelphia. Economic circumstances made this impossible, and he ended up on a railroad re-
pair gang in North Carolina. Finding this to
be the equivalent of "slave labor," Semlek
fled to Canada and then went West. He was
given 320 acres of land in Wyoming, which he
developed successfully. For this, he obtained
an additional 240 acres for development. Other Estonians soon appeared in the location,
Moorcroft. Even as late as the 1940s there
was still a colony of 60 Estonians in Moorcroft, including children. The most successful settler here was Semlek, who by the 1950s
owned 4,108 acres of farmland.

March. The Töömees (Workingman), a socialist
paper in the Estonian language, began publication three times a month in Oakland, California. The editors and publishers were M.
Koffer, G. Tammik and A. Põder. The paper
could not secure adequate financial backing,
however, and it ceased publication in the
summer of 1908. One of the editors, Koffer
[Coffer], subsequently became a wealthy buil-
der and was named Honorary Consul of the Republic of Estonia in San Francisco.

1908   A Philadelphia Estonian Society was established. In 1910 a section split off and
joined the Socialist Party to form the core
of the Philadelphia Estonian Workers Club,
founded in 1926.

An airship built by an Estonian named Ots
failed to take off in San Francisco. The
trouble was apparently in the weight of the
gondola, which pulled the middle section of
the airship to the ground after it had risen
and tore the cloth containing the gas. Also,
the airship had been built without separating
chambers. The gondola contained a car engine
geared to move the dirigible. A photo shows
it with the rear end on top of a building and

the other end down on the street below. Ots,
who had sold shares to finance this flying
venture, disappeared without a trace.

1909   An Estonian Society was established in Port-
        land, Oregon. The following year it was re-
        named the Portland Estonian Section of the
        Socialist Party of America.

        John Nernof attracted considerable attention
        in the New York press by driving a steam en-
        gine car, which he himself had built, in Cen-
        tral Park. Nernof, born in 1882 in Estonia,
        was a ship's mechanic by trade. He was quite
        active in New York Estonian society at the
        time.

        Anton Hanson, born in Estonia in 1879, was
        one of the designing architects of the Seattle
        World's Fair and was awarded a grand prize.
        Hanson arrived in the country in 1906 and was
        a contributor to the Estonian socialist news-
        paper Uus Ilm (The New World) in New York. He
        also participated in the 1915 San Francisco
        and 1916 San Diego exhibitions. Later, he
        settled in Alberta, Canada.

        January. At the initiative of the Central
        Committee of the American Estonian Socialist
        Association, a meeting was called in New
        York to establish a new Estonian newspaper.
        Other organizations which participated inclu-
        ded the New York Estonian Beneficial Society
        and the Society Lootus (Hope). A total of
        150 people attended the meeting and 100 of
        them bought shares in the new American-Esto-
        nian Publishing Corporation, which was to
        publish a new Estonian-language newspaper,
        Uus Ilm (The New World).

        June. The first issue of the new Estonian
        weekly newspaper, Uus Ilm (The New World), ap-
        peared under the editorship of Peeter Speek.
        A former socialist editor in Estonia, Speek
        went into exile after the 1905 Revolution
        and arrived in the United States in 1908. The
        task of the newspaper, according to him, was
        "the education of the working class and the
        interpretation of events." Speek remained as
        editor for a year and was replaced by Linda
        Jürmann, wife and companion of Eduard Vilde.
        The latter was well on his way to becoming
        one of the best-known Estonian writers. Vilde,

who followed Jürmann to America, was detained
on Ellis Island for a month because someone
had denounced him as an "anarchist" and a
"bigamist". This was to make a lasting impression on Vilde concerning America.

In 1911 Jürmann and Vilde left the United States and Hans Pöögelmann became the new
editor of Uus Ilm. From then on the newspaper became increasingly Marxist in orientation. After the 1917 Revolution in Russia,
and some squabbling over editorial policy in
the 1920s, Uus Ilm became the organ of Estonian-American communists. It has continued
as such ever since. As time went on, the
publication was issued less frequently, and
presently it is a monthly. Its circulation
was never large: 700 subscribers during
World War One, 600 during the 1920s, and 350
in the 1950s. Matters have not improved
since then. In its January, 1971, issue Uus
Ilm appealed for direct financial support
from its subscribers. The building which
housed its printing press in New York's Harlem had been abandoned by its owner and was
scheduled for demolition by the city. "Workers of all countries," comments Uus Ilm
editorially, "have never been as close as now
to their ultimate goal -- socialism... Therefore, comrades, once more -- hands into our
wallets, everyone helping as best they can to
achieve this goal which is dear to us." But
despite its present difficulties, Uus Ilm
does have the distinction of being the oldest
continuously published Estonian-language periodical in the United States.

August. Uus Ilm, the New York Estonian socialist newspaper, reported that there were
3,000 Estonians in the United States. A total of 147 Estonians were members of four
socialist organizations, 56 of them in New
York and the remainder in San Francisco,
Bankhead and Seattle.

December 25. The Ameerika Eesti Postimees,
published by Reverend Rebane, reported that
on Christmas Day the Boston Eesti Vabameelne
Selts (Estonian Freethinking Society) held
its very first social event, in Cambridge,
Massachusetts, to which a number of Finnish
"guys" and "dolls" also were invited. An ob-
server wrote: "Oh what pleasure and joy
there was when the Society's Chairman, Mr.

Mõtus, with tiny Miss Minna Danner and Mr.
Sipelgas with the huge Miss Leontine Allemann,
with pale faces, hollow cheeks and sunken
eyes, swirled about dancing. And 'black Judas' Mr. Seiman 'side split' with a Finnish
'gal' and Mr. Laas, whose wife is back home,
cuddled up to the girls. And men were dancing
with lasses and others' wives pressed against
their breasts. Even 'Amor' was here with his
mail and worked so hard that the little fellow was sweating all over. And this cost the
participants a mere thirty-five cents." In
the following year the Boston Estonian Freethinking Society changed its name to Boston
Estonian Socialist Association.

1915   A Seattle-Tacoma Estonian Socialist Associa-
        tion was established. It had about 40 mem-
        bers, and in 1919 it joined the American Com-
        munist Party. The latter underwent reorgani-
        zation in 1926, abolishing its federated eth-
        nic units. The result was the creation of
        the Seattle Estonian Workers Club with 24
        members.

1916   Anarhist (The Anarchist), an Estonian monthly
        issued by the California Matsiselts (Peasant
        Association), appeared for a short period.

        Ameerika Ristirahva Leht (The American Chris-
        tians Newspaper), a mimeographed and subse-
        quently home-typeset small-format newsletter,
        was published for about a year by Reverend
        Conrad Klemmer. A locksmith and tinkerer by
        earlier training, Klemmer arrived in the Uni-
        ted States in 1907. He became a lay preacher
        to about 50 Estonians in San Francisco and
        soon met a professor who talked him into tak-
        ing up a religious calling. He studied at
        Concord Theological Seminary in Springfield,
        Illinois, and was ordained in 1911. He was
        initially assigned to a Finnish congregation
        in Arizona. It was not until 1913 that he
        began to preach regularly in Estonian, becom-
        ing the successor to Reverend Hans Rebane,
        who had died in 1911.

        September. A New York Estonian Sports Socie-
        ty was formed. The following spring it was
        renamed the Estonian G. Lurich and A. Aberg
        Athletic Club. Georg Lurich and Aleksander
        Aberg were among the world's most outstanding
        wrestlers at the time and their matches took

place in Madison Square Garden. Another Estonian world wrestling champion, Georg
Hackenschmidt, also competed in America between 1908 and 1911. By 1919 the Club had
more than 100 members. Since there were professional wrestlers among its members, it
joined the American Athletic Union and changed
its name to the Estonian-American Athletic
Club.

1918   The New York Estonian Socialist Association
joined the Communist Labor Party as one of
its subdivisions.

February 24. Estonia was declared an independent Republic, and Estonian-Americans began to work intensively for American recognition of their country of origin and to assist
in providing material aid.

September. An American-Esthonian League was
established to promote the recognition of the
newly declared independent Republic of Esto-
nia.The founding members were Julius Sarei,
Otto Kaaparin, Jakob Laht, Gustav Wentzel,
Jüri Copelman, Charles Murley and Ivan Narodny
[Jaan Sibul]. The league published a political, commercial, literary and scholarly periodical, Esthonia, which appeared during 1919
and 1920. It was also responsible for obtaining two million dollars worth of aid for Estonia from the American Red Cross.

1919   The New York Estonian Baptist Congregation
was established at 235 East 83rd Street. Between 1918 and 1923 an Estonian printer and
preacher, John Felsberg, issued a newspaper
with a Baptist orientation, Ameerika Teekäija
(The American Wanderer).

May. The League of Esthonians, Letts, Lithuanians and Ukrainians of America held a mass
rally at Carnegie Hall for the independence
of their countries. There were 5,000 people
crowded inside, with many others left outside.
Commander Grafton Beall of the United States
Navy spoke on behalf of the Estonians. The
American-Esthonian League delegated Hans L.
Pymson and Peeter A. Pabstel to be Estonian
representatives to the League of Esthonians,
Letts, Lithuanians and Ukrainians, with Pymson becoming the vice-president of this organization. The league was formed to "aid the

American people and the American Government
in reaching a better understanding of the
political, economic and social conditions in
Eastern Europe;" to induce the United States
Government and the Allies to recognize the
sovereignty of Estonia and the other countries; to aid the four republics from aggression and invasion; and to further trade and
commerce between them and the United States.

THE INTERWAR YEARS 1922-1939 AND THE WAR YEARS 1940-1945

1922-1939: YEARS OF RETRENCHMENT

1922-
1929

Estonian organizational life in New York was
pretty much in disarray during this period.
The Estonian-American communists had achieved
control of the New York Estonian Society in
1917, and they also came close to dominating
the Estonian-American Athletic Club, which
basically strove to keep out of politics al-
together. The only other Estonian organization in New York during these years was the
American Esthonian League, which lobbied for
American recognition of Estonia, but it went
out of existence in 1922. In December of
1922 a politically neutral New York Estonian
Society Edu (Success) was created. Its membership grew rapidly to several hundred. Among
the leading members were the following: H.
Copelman, C. Murley, Mr. and Mrs. Augustus
Pierce, Mr. and Mrs. Andres Pranspill, H.
Leoke, Martin Lauer, and A. Waldman. An
American Estonian Music Club went its separate
way in 1925, soon to be followed by a New
York Estonian Club, the membership of which
was made up of young intellectuals. Also, in
1924 there appeared on the scene a politically oriented and predominantly socialist Pro-
gressive Estonian Society Kiir (Ray), and in
1928 the communist New York Estonian Workers
Club. The main purpose of the Society Kiir
was to support the Estonian-language newspaper Uus Ilm (see page 11). In the spring of
1928 all of these diverse organizations supported a fund-raising social event to assist
the Estonian Olympic Committee in participating in the Olympic Games and to launch a
second Estonian newspaper in New York. A total of 700 Estonians were present in a spirit
of conciliation. Plans were laid to establish a joint "Estonian Home" for all organi-

zations. However, the divisions were too
deep to permit such a plan to materialize,
and the goals of unity were realized only
partially. All but the communists joined to
establish the Estonian Educational Society,
initially named United Estonian Society, in
the fall of 1929. The society has served
as an umbrella organization for most Estonian activities in the New York area since.
The board members in 1929 were: K. Saar, O.
Kukepuu, A. Lootus, R. Vaino, and C. Kusik.
The Estonian Educational Society was located
in Harlem until 1946. Since then, its home
has been the Estonian House, 243 East 34th
Street, in Manhattan. (See Document No. 2.)

1922   A Baltic-American Society was organized in
New York by the American Friends of Lithuania,
Latvia and Esthonia. Robert J. Caldwell was
named president of the organization and Hans
Leoke, acting consul of Estonia, was elected
one of the three honorary presidents. Reverend Conrad Klemmer and Dr. Peter Speek,
both Estonian-born, were on the executive
committee and among the directors, respectively. The purposes of the society included the
development of friendship between the peoples
of the Baltic republics and the United States,
the promotion of Baltic culture in America,
and the furthering of economic, commercial and
educational ties. The society was headquartered at 15 Park Row, and annual membership
fees ranged from five dollars per year for
contributing members, who had no voting
rights, to twenty-five dollars for associate
members. A one-time fee of five-hundred dollars was required of patrons.

A San Francisco Estonian Section of the Communist Labor Party was established. A social
event it held soon thereafter attracted 267.
The section was restructured into the San
Francisco Estonian Workers Club in June,
1927, with an initial membership of 20.

July 28. The United States accorded diplomatic recognition to the Republic of Estonia and
the other two Baltic States, Latvia and Lithuania. American-Estonians had worked hard to
achieve this. For example, in 1921 a delegation of four representatives -- Conrad Klemmer, J.W. Tiedeberg, C. Flink and Isaac Mik-
kal -- presented a petition to President Har-

ding on behalf of the Estonian-American community, calling for the recognition of Estonia. The first Estonian envoy to the United States was Professor Ants Piip, who was welcomed by the Estonian-American community of New York on December 25, 1923. Estonia's leading authority on international law, Piip later was a visiting professor at the University of California at Los Angeles and lectured to organizations such as the Brookings Institution in Washington, D.C. At one point, Piip was Estonia's Head of State (Riigivanem).

1923   Fall. A Boston Estonian Workers Cultural Society was founded with a membership of 40. The name was soon changed to the Boston Estonian Workers Club.

1924   April. In determining immigration quotas for various countries, the United States Congress calculated that there were 5,100 people in America of Estonian ancestry in 1890; 16,855 in 1900; 44,900 in 1910; and 69,200 in 1920. The Estonian quota was affixed at 116; that is, 116 people born in Estonia could immigrate to the United States in any one year. During the 1920s and 1930s, however, even this small annual quota was not used up. In the 1920s the American specialist on immigration, John D. Trevor, published a number of articles on the quotas, and in his last work he asserted that in 1920 there was a total of 200,230 people in the United States of Estonian ancestry.

1925   March. The first issue of a new Estonian-language newspaper, Ameerika Eestlane (The American Estonian), appeared in New York. The editor was Peeter Leoke. However, after six months it went out of business.

1926   September 19. The Detroit Estonian Society Kodu (Home) was founded, with Jüri Rees [Riis] elected chairman. It is still active currently.

1928   April. Still another attempt was made to issue a new Estonian-language newspaper in New York. Anton Heilman began to publish the New Yorgi Eestlane (The New York Estonian), but it appeared only for about six months.

May 6. The New York Estonian Workers Club
was established. By 1932 it had about 200
members and supported a choir, a music circle,
a sports circle, and Estonian Youth Club. An
autonomous Art Association was founded on
December 10, 1936, and it soon affiliated itself with the Artists' Union.

Summer. A South California Estonian Society
was established. Among the founders were
Charles Kodil and Peter Tobi, who arrived in
Los Angeles in 1913. The name was subsequently changed to Los Angeles Estonian Society. At a general meeting in 1953 Charles
Kodil was made an honorary member, together
with Charles K. Janson, Martha Janson, Peeter
Leoke and George A. Alexius. The society today owns an Estonian House in Los Angeles,
which is the center of Estonian-American activity in the region.

1929   This year saw the publication in the United
States of three works by Count Hermann von
Keyserling: The Recovery of Truth; America
Set Free; and Creative Understanding. Another of his books, The Travel Diary of a Phi-
losopher, was published in 1935. Keyserling,
born in Estonia in 1880, studied at the Universities of Dorpat (Tartu), Heidelberg and
Vienna. He left Estonia for Germany in 1918.
The following year he married the granddaugh-
ter of Count Otto von Bismarck. In 1920 he
opened the School of Wisdom in Darmstadt,
Germany, with the purpose of regenerating
mankind after World War One. He lectured
extensively in the United States during the
1930s on spiritual renewal.

1930   February 9. An Estonian Club was founded in
Chicago, with J. Olep as chairman and A.
Sandluk as vice-chairman. E. Judas was the
first secretary and V. Reinvald the first
treasurer. The Club had an initial membership of 18. Today, the Chicago Estonian-
American community is a very active one, and
one of the largest in the country. It has
its own Estonian House, several congregations, and sponsors a number of ethnic organizations.

April 2. An Estonian Society of San Francisco was established with John Rehe as
chairman. Other leading members included

John Ostrat and Ernst Jaakson. Although the
society foundered after a number of years, it
was reconstituted with Ostrat as chairman in
1949. Jaakson served subsequently as consul
in the Estonian legation in New York City.
Upon the death of Consul General Johannes Kaiv
in 1965, Jaakson was recognized as the consul
general of the Republic of Estonia in the United States by the American government. The
Estonian Society of San Francisco which he
had initially helped to form is today a vigorous organization.

December 18. Two Estonian brothers crossed
the Atlantic in a 29-foot sailboat and arrived
in Miami. Kōu and Ahto Walter, aged 23 and
18, respectively, had left Tallinn, Estonia,
on August 7. The idea of crossing the Atlantic was that of the younger brother. On their
last 4,000-mile stretch from the Canary Islands to the United States mainland, they were
joined by a Canadian, C.P. Barber. The total
mileage of their voyage was 7,000. They received a tremendous welcome in the United
States. An Estonian publication commented:
"With their overcourageous journey the young
men have given Estonia better publicity than
any diplomatic representative." Ahto Walter
authored a book about his experiences, Racing
the Seas, published by Farrar and Rinehart in
New York in 1935. In 1945 Kōu Walter and his
family returned to the United States on a "Viking boat" across the Atlantic as political
refugees. In 1968 Ahto Walter decided to sell
his supermarkets and other real estate holdings on the Virgin Islands, where he had settled, bought a fishing boat and set out to sea
to fish near the African coast.

1931   June 23. A well-known Estonian writer, Andres
            Saal, died in Hollywood, California. Born in
            1861 in Estonia, his books -- such as Vambola,
            Leili and Uudu ja Meta -- were very well re-
            ceived in his native land. In 1898 he joined
            the service of the Dutch government and went
            to Java [Indonesia] as a topographer. In the
            early 1920s he moved to California, where he
            continued to write.

            October. Meie Tee (Our Path), a new Estonian
            monthly, began publication. The editorial
            board of the first issue was composed of A.
            Koovits, E. Derrik, R. Ratsep, C. Kusik and

A. Tamm, with August Waldman as business
manager. It was sponsored by the Art and
Literature Department of the Estonian Educational Society in New York. The periodical
has appeared regularly to date.

1932   Elvy Kaalep came to the United States in 1932
to fly across the Atlantic, but she was beat-
en to the punch by Amelia Earhart by three
days. Instead, she became a doll manufactur-
er, employing no less than 60 female workers.
World War One had found her in the Far East,
where she graduated from a commercial high
school. Born in Pärnu, Estonia, she returned
to her homeland in 1926. Eager to fly, Elvy
Kaalep obtained a private pilot's license in
Germany in 1931. After her abortive attempt
to cross the Atlantic, she wrote a children's
book, Air Babies, which sold 100,000 copies.
Her special doll, a creation in a flying suit
equipped with a parachute, was an instant
success. Having retired to Florida in the
1970s, Elvy Kaalep is still busy, producing
leather-mosaic "pictures" for home decorative
purposes.

1933   The New York Estonian monthly Meie Tee estimated that there were 54,000 Estonians in
North America. In the United States the
largest concentration, a presumed 12,000
people, was in the New York metropolitan
area. The Atlantic seaboard rated a total
estimate of 17,000 while the number in California was placed at 5,000. Information
was provided on Estonian settlements as follows: Irma and Gleason, Wisconsin (20
farms); Dundee (near Salem) and Rose Lodge,
Oregon (about 22 farms); Snohomish, Washington (6 farms); and Moorcroft, Wyoming (7
farms).

May. The first North American Estonian Congress was held in New York on May 26, 1933.
The congress decided to found an American-
Estonian League and elected J. Annusson as
its chairman. The purpose of the league was
to organize American-Estonians under its auspices. The New York Estonian monthly, Meie
Tee, was unanimously declared the organ of
the league.

1936   Carl Sundbach, born in 1888 in Estonia, in-
vented a freezer which reduced the bulk

freezing of fish to one-third of the time required previously. Sundbach, a mechanical engineer, came to the United States in 1909. He was active in the Socialist Party before World War One. In 1936 he was one of the founders of the Boston Estonian Society.

January 12. The Baltimore Estonian Society was established. On February 2 it elected the following officers: John Roosman, secretary; Albert Miller, treasurer; and John Reiman, Ivan Luht and Evald Moses, trustees. The society was incorporated in 1945, and within a year, had 100 members. During the immediate postwar years the society was quite active in sponsoring and otherwise assisting Estonian refugees to this country and in working on behalf of self-determination for Soviet-annexed Estonia. By 1950, its membership had risen to 225. Baltimore will be the site of the Second Estonian World Festival in 1976. (See Document No. 20.)

April. The Boston Estonian Society was established with the following board members: Dr. E. Ein, Ludvig Juht, A. Pillman, C. Sundbach and Rokenbaum. One of its first events was a concert by the contrabass soloist of the Boston Symphony Orchestra, Ludvig Juht. In addition, his wife, Amanda Juht, a soprano, sang Estonian folk songs. The society is still active presently, its leadership in the hands of post-World War Two immigrants.

July 4. Estonian-born Hardy Nurmsen undertook a 7,500-mile journey by canoe. The itinerary took him up the Hudson River from New York, then by way of the Erie Canal and the Great Lakes to Chicago, down the Mississippi to the Gulf of Mexico, from there to Florida, and finally back up the East Coast to New York. The journey took a year and a half to complete and was subject to considerable publicity. Nurmsen subsequently wrote a book about his trip, Süstaga läbi Ameerika (Through America by Canoe), which was published in Estonia.

1938   Soprano Miliza Korjus was at work at MGM Studios in Hollywood in her starring role in The Great Waltz, a film based on the life of Johann Strauss. The movie and Korjus' role in it received world-wide acclaim. The sin-

ger-actress' father was Estonian and her mother was Polish, and she hails from the Estonian
capital, Tallinn. Prior to coming to the United States, Korjus was with the Berlin State
Opera. She later settled in California, continuing her singing career and making records,
both of which have been well received.

A photo exhibit by Arthur Ermates was held in
Washington, D.C. Ermates was born in Tallinn
in 1896 and arrived in the United States via
the Far East in 1922. He settled in Hollywood, California, where he worked as a movie
actor and took up photography on the side. He
soon began to specialize in photo portraits
and his subjects included numerous actors and
movie stars, including Douglas Fairbanks Sr.,
Myrna Loy, Charles Farrel, Franchot Tone, Cor-
nelia Otis Skinner and Richard Bennett.

February 24. The twentieth anniversary of the
independence of the Republic of Estonia was
celebrated in New York. NBC, through forty
affiliates, carried a program on Estonia which
included an address by Karl Kuusik, Estonian
consul in New York, and a concert performance
by pianist Vladimir Padwa and contrabassist
Ludvig Juht. A recorded message in Estonian
by the president of Estonia, Konstantin Päts,
was broadcast by New York City's WNYC in the
early evening. The day was concluded with a
festive meeting at Columbia University.

April. Following the guidelines of the Seventh Congress of the Communist International
in Moscow on united front tactics, Mihkel
Nukk, editor of Uus Ilm, the New York Estonian communist newpaper, attempted to unite
all Estonian-American organizations "to work
out a program in defense of the Estonian people's independence and self-determination in
view of the danger that Estonia faces from a
fascist threat." On April 21 the following
convened at New York's Pythian Hall: Mihkel
Nukk and A. Mackie, representing the Estonian
Workers Clubs League; J. Kari and H. Kaaman,
representing the Lurich and Aberg Athletic
Club; and E. Kuningas and B. Eistrat, representing the New York Estonian Workers Club.
Also present were representatives of the Association of Estonian Independence War Veterans in New York. The latter made a series of
demands for changes in the editorial policy

of Uus Ilm, and the attempt at achieving a
united Estonian-American front under communist
leadership foundered on this issue. No subsequent such attempt has been made.

1939   The following Estonian-American organizations
were active during 1939: the American-Estonian League in New York, founded in 1933; the
New York Estonian Educational Society, founded
in 1929, the Estonian Society Arendaja in
Cleveland, founded in 1925; the Detroit Estonian Society Kodu, founded in 1925; the Boston
Estonian Society, founded in 1936; the Estonian Association of Washington, D.C., founded in
1937; and the South California Estonian Society, founded in 1928. Additionally, under the
wing of the American-Estonian Workers Clubs
League there was a number of Workers Clubs
and affiliated organizations in New York, Boston, Philadelphia, Baltimore, Cleveland, El-
mont (Long Island), Seattle and San Francisco.
Finally, there were three active congregations: the Estonian Evangelical Lutheran
Church in New York, founded in 1898; the Estonian Baptist Church, also in New York, founded
in 1919; and the Estonian Pentecostal Church,
again in New York, founded in 1928. (See Documents No. 3 and 4.)

Spring. William M. Leiserson was appointed a
member of the Labor Arbitration Commission by
President Franklin D. Roosevelt. Leiserson
was born in Tallinn, Estonia, and arrived in
the United States at the age of seven in 1890.
He studied at the University of Wisconsin and
obtained his Ph.D. from Columbia University in
1911. He had been employed earlier by the Department of Labor.

THE WAR YEARS: 1940-1945

1940   March. Voldemar Rannus' bas-relief of Albert
Ely Beach was dedicated at the subway station
near New York City Hall. Beach was the father
of the New York subway system. Rannus' sculptures were shown at the New York's World Fair
and are currently on exhibit in locations such
as the Brooklyn Museum. Interestingly, his
work Negro Figure is on display at the Moscow
Museum of Western Art. Rannus, born in Estonia in 1880, died in New York on November 26,
1944. He arrived in the United States in 1905

and studied at the National Academy of Design
in New York and subsequently in Paris and
Rome.

June-July. The Republic of Estonia was occupied by the Soviet Army and lost its independence through forced incorporation into the
Soviet Union. Most Western countries did not
recognize the Soviet annexation of Estonia.
The United States protest was vigorous. (See
Document No. 5.) The Estonian-American community actively participated in the call for
non-recognition of the Soviet aggression and
took immediate measures to assist the refugees
from Soviet-occupied Estonia.

Summer. Estonian diplomats in America and
leaders of the Estonian-American community decided to form an organization of international
scope, the Ülemaailmne Eesti Ühing (World Association of Estonians). Its purpose was to
coordinate the political struggle to free Estonia from Soviet rule, and its first president was the Estonian diplomat Johannes Markus.
The association worked intensively for Estonian interests, especially within the United
States, and additionally provided informational services in regard to the situation in Estonia. The association was subsequently instrumental in creating the Estonian American
National Council in 1952, which took over most
of its activities within the United States.

1941   June 15. Governor Herbert H. Lehman of New
York proclaimed "Baltic States Day". Special
services and prayers were held at the Cathedral of St. John the Divine and at St. Patrick's Cathedral in New York. Services were
officiated, respectively, by Bishops Manning
and Spellman. This was followed by a rally
at Town Hall under the chairmanship of Ben
Howe. The rally adopted a number of resolutions which were forwarded to Washington.
Lehman was the first governor of any state to
issue such a proclamation. (See Documents
No. 6 and 7.)

July 3. In response to inquiries addressed
to the Department of State by J. Kaiv, the
diplomatic representative of the Republic of
Estonia in the United States, A.A. Berle, assistant secretary of state, assured Kaiv that
the American government continued to recognize

him as Estonian Consul General in charge of
legation.   The communication also added that
the United States does not recognize the ab-
sorption of Estonia by the Soviet Union. American nonrecognition of the annexation of the
Baltic states by the Soviet Union has continued to the present day. (See Documents No.
5 and 17.)

August 14.   The Estonian-American community
laid the groundwork for a central relief organization.   The idea originated with an Estonian diplomat, Johannes Markus, who at the
time was president of the World Association
of Estonians. At a meeting of the association
on this date he stated, in part: "The German-
Russian war is devastating our homeland. Thousands have been left without shelter, people
are threatened by destitution and starvation,
they have nowhere to turn for help..." As a
remedy, Markus proposed the formation of a
special committee which would collect clothing
and other items, and at an opportune moment,
send these to Estonia.
        The association decided at the meeting to
found an Estonian Committee for Assistance.
On September 3 the association named the committee the Estonian Relief Committee. And on
October 31 the committee was officially incorporated in the State of New York with Salme
Kaiv, wife of the Estonian Consul General in
the United States, as chairwoman.
        Within the month the committee had raised
$1,151 in donations, this from only nine indi-
viduals. At first it was not possible to send
assistance directly to Estonia because of the
war. However, when the first Estonian political refugees began to arrive in Sweden, the
committee immediately dispatched $5,000 to as-
sist them. Assistance was also provided to
several Estonians detained by immigration authorities at Ellis Island, and to those who
arrived in the several "Viking boats" between
1945 and 1951. However, the committee's most
important achievement in the postwar years was
related to the resettlement of Estonian refugees from the displaced persons camps in Germany. Between 1948 and 1952 the committee
found homes and sponsors for 7,336 Estonians
wishing to immigrate to the United States, a
number equal to about 60-percent of the group
coming here.
        In recent years the committee has contin-

ued its activities at an intense pace. It
has provided assistance to needy Estonians in
the United States, sent monetary and material
support to needy Estonians in Western Europe,
sponsored children's camps in West Germany,
contributed appreciably to the building and
operation of a Disabled Estonian Veterans
Home in West Germany, and in conjunction with
other Estonian relief organizations, sent
packages to Estonians deported by Soviet authorities to Siberia. Between 1941 and 1973
the committee had seen $600,000 go through
its treasury. Since most of the administra-
tive labor needed to operate the committee
has been voluntarily donated, the greater part
of the above sum went directly to mutual aid
programs. Also noteworthy is the fact that
most of the committee's financial resources
have been donations from the Estonian-Americans themselves, although other contributions
have been made by the National Catholic Welfare Conference and the William Zimdin Foundation in California. Zimdin was an American
businessman born in Estonia.

1942   John [Johan] Triesault was given a major role
in Michael Curtis's film Mission to Moscow
(Warner Brothers Pictures). Triesault, who
was born on the Estonian island of Hiiumaa,
had his first acting job as an extra with the
Metropolitan Opera in 1917. This was followed
by appearances on Broadway. After his movie
debut he became typecast as the "Prussian of-
ficer," and he has appeared in numerous mo-
tion pictures in that particular role.

May. Theodore Alexis Wiel was presented the
honorary degree of Doctor of Laws by American
International College in Springfield, Massachusetts. Born in Estonia in 1893, Wiel went
to sea in 1910. In 1912 he settled in New
York and studied at the American International
College from 1914 to 1917. He volunteered
for the U.S. Army during World War One and
fought in France, where he was wounded twice.
Wiel was awarded the Silver Star with Oak Leaf
Cluster for gallantry in action. After the
war he went back to sea but soon returned to
college, obtaining a Master of Arts degree
from Clark University in 1931 and a doctoral
degree in international relations subsequently. In 1932 he joined the faculty of American International College, and in 1942 he be-

came its Dean. Wiel was the Republican can-
didate for mayor of Springfield in 1953.

1944   The World Association of Estonians bought
                $13,500 worth of United States War Bonds. The
                money, in turn, was used to purchase six am-
                bulances for the U.S. Army. Each ambulance
                bore the following sign: "Field Ambulance,
                Presented to the United States Army by the
                World Association of Estonians through the
                purchase of War Bonds". (See Document No. 8.)

THE ARRIVAL OF THE REFUGEES AND BEYOND: 1945-1974

1945-   Although some 30,000 Estonian citizens depart-
1974   ed or fled their country between 1939 and
                1943, a single large massive flight occurred
                in the fall of 1944, as Soviet armies were
                about to reenter Estonia. The Soviet Union
                had already annexed Estonia in 1940, but its
                rule was interrupted by three years of German
                occupation. One large group of Estonians fled
                in 1944 to Sweden, crossing a stormy Baltic
                Sea in small boats. A somewhat larger group
                fled overland as well as by sea toward Germa-
                ny. As World War Two drew to a close, there
                were about 100,000 Estonians, or 9-percent of
                the prewar population, in various Western
                countries. Within a few years they were scat-
                tered around the world through various reset-
                tlement programs, refusing to return to Esto-
                nia while it was under Soviet rule. Most of
                the Estonians arriving in America after 1945
                came from refugee camps in Germany, although
                some came by way of Sweden.
                     The fact that most in the currently active
                Estonian-American community are political ex-
                iles has had a profound impact on the life of
                the group. Thus, many of the organizations
                which were established from 1940 onward were
                political ones directed at fighting Soviet
                rule in Estonia. Since elements of the group
                were scattered world-wide, many of these or-
                ganizations were international in scope. The
                sense of political mission, the necessity for
                a global struggle, had an effect also on other
                aspects of group life. Thus, in the early
                post-war years a heavy emphasis was placed on
                maintaining Estonian culture in exile because
                the heavy hand of Stalin's rule led to cultu-
                ral repression within Estonia. Indeed, the
                fact of exile saw the appearance of two new

dimensions as to what being Estonian was all
about: that of pagulus and that of välisvõitlus. The former term refers to the condition or state of political exile with its
many cultural, national and political ramifi-
cations. In a literal sense, the latter term
means "the struggle from abroad." It encom-
passes all types of activity, essentially political in nature, which are designed to free
Estonia from Soviet rule.

In any case, the two concepts, pagulus
and välisvõitlus, provided the ideological
base which accounted for two significant
characteristics of the Estonian-American community. These were the high degree of organization and the interrelationship of Estonian-Americans to other Estonians, from Australia to Sweden, that is, the international nature of their ethnicity.

Not all of either characteristic can be
fully explained, of course, as a consequence
of exile. Thus, the preceding parts of this
book indicated that at the turn of the century Estonian-Americans were already highly
"organized." Also, an international flavor
as to what it meant to be Estonian had been
provided by the fact that the war, and later
resettlement, split many families and friends
who naturally maintained contacts. And when
Estonian refugees first began forming organizations, it was natural to build on those
which had already existed in Estonia. Thus,
old organizations were reconstituted outside
Estonia by their members and because the members had settled in many different countries,
the reconstituted organizations were by de-
fault international in scope. And finally,
an international context had been provided to
"Estonianism" even earlier by the Välis Eesti
(Estonia Abroad) movement of the prewar period, which strove to unite Estonians world
wide in terms of cultural identity with the
Estonian homeland through an organization
based in Tallinn, the Estonian capital. This
movement was, in fact, successful. It ex-
plains in part the interest which the prewar
Estonian-Americans exhibited during the war
years in events in their country of origin.

The concepts of pagulus and välisvõitlus
are such that they explain a good deal of the
nature of Estonian-American society from 1945
through the late 1960s. From then on a
younger generation has begun to explore new

avenues for the expression of its ethnicity,
which in the mid-1970s, however, has changed
more in form than in content.

THE LATE 1940s: ARRIVAL OF THE REFUGEES

1945   This year was the beginning of the Estonian
                "Viking boat" immigration era to the United
                States. When it appeared that Swedish au-
                thorities might forcibly repatriate some Es-
                tonian and other Baltic refugees to the So-
                viet Union, it caused fear throughout the
                group. As a consequence, several hundred Es-
                tonians decided to depart for the New World,
                mostly in 30 and 40-foot vessels, even though
                they did not have immigration visas. Thirty-
                four such boats made the trans-Atlantic voy-
                age between 1945 and 1951, most of them ar-
                riving in Florida in 1945 and 1946. The num-
                ber of passengers, including crew, varied
                from 6 to 69. Since they arrived in the Uni-
                ted States without proper visas, it took some
                time before they could legally become perma-
                nent residents. In 1951 and 1952, Senator
                Herbert H. Lehman of New York was active in
                the enactment of special legislation designed
                to aid these immigrants. (See Documents No.
                11 and 12.)

                December 20. Among the first Estonian "Vik-
                ing boats" to arrive in the United States was
                the Erma, which docked in Norfolk, Virginia,
                just before Christmas. One of the individu-
                als arriving with the Erma, Voldemar Veedam,
                wrote a book, Sailing to Freedom, about his
                adventures. The work appeared in several
                English-language editions and was translated
                into seventeen other languages. (See Docu-
                ment No. 10.)

1946   There were many Estonian "war brides," and
                most of them managed easily to come to the
                United States to join their returning GI-
                husbands. Dolly A. Nelson was the exception.
                It was not until July 8, 1952, six years af-
                ter she married a San Franciscan, Sergeant
                H. Nelson, in Germany, that she set foot on
                American soil, arriving in New York with her
                five-year old daughter. Soon after her mar-
                riage, Mrs. Nelson had decided to visit her
                parents in East Germany. She was arrested
                by East German authorities together with her

father and for four years they were held
prisoner in various locations, including the
former concentration camp, Buchenwald. Her
daughter was born in captivity in 1946, perhaps the only American citizen to have been
born in a prison camp behind the Iron Curtain. Mrs. Nelson was born in Tallinn, Estonia. Eventually, she, her father, mother,
and daughter all got out of East Germany.

February 27. Augustus Pierce, president of
the New York Estonian Educational Society
since 1932, died. Pierce, born in Estonia
in 1885, arrived in the United States in 1907.
He was initially active in the New York Estonian Socialist Association and, later, during
the 1920s, in the Estonian Society Edu, which
he also headed.

June. The Lakewood, New Jersey, Estonian Association, founded a year ago, placed the
corner-stone to a building on grounds donated
by a local Estonian-American farmer for an
Estonian House. The cornerstone box contained an Estonian flag, a copy of the association's charter, the latest issue of the
New York Estonian monthly Meie Tee, issues of
other Estonian newspapers from Europe, and a
handful of soil from the farm of the president of the Estonian Republic, Konstantin
Päts.
       The Lakewood Estonian community had its
beginnings in the 1930s when a number of families moved to the area, many of them taking
up poultry farming. Additional Estonian families arrived after World War Two. By the
late 1960s there were approximately 600 Estonians in the Lakewood area, and the Lakewood
Estonian Association grew to about 300 members. In spite of its relatively small size,
the association has been one of the most active in the country. The Estonian House and
its grounds have hosted numerous cultural and
social events, as well as annual Estonian
Athletic Games, for the whole eastern seaboard, drawing up to 3,000 participants. An
Estonian Lutheran congregation founded in
1948 erected its own church in 1964, and more
recently the community built a facility for
the Estonian Archives in the United States
next to the church. Lastly, the community
has been primary caretaker of the Estonian
Scouting Reservation located in neighboring

Jackson Township. Many of the postwar Lakewood Estonians entered the building trades,
some of them forming sizable construction
companies. Almost all of the work necessary
to build the Estonian House, the Lutheran
church, and the archives and to develop the
scouting reservation was accomplished through
the donation of materials and labor by members of the Lakewood Estonian-American community. (See Document No. 15.)

1947   October 11. An Estonian House was dedicated
                in New York City. Virtually all Estonian or-
                ganizations in the area soon operated from
                under its roof. It is still located at 243
                East 34th Street, New York, N.Y. 10016.

1948-   In 1948 the United States Congress enacted
1952   the Displaced Persons Act to assist in the
                resettlement of European refugees. Under the
                provisions of the act 10,427 persons born in
                Estonia were allowed to immigrate to the Uni-
                ted States during the five-year period 1948-
                1952. In Estonian-American history this was
                the highest known concentration of immigra-
                tion. 1950 was the peak year with 5,422 per-
                sons born in Estonia arriving in the country.
                The first ship to bring displaced persons to
                American shores was the General Black, arriv-
                ing on October 30, 1948. Among those aboard
                were 14 Estonians. The last displaced person
                admitted under the act was Heino Heinla, born
                in Tallinn, Estonia, in 1923. (See Table 1 in
                the Appendix.)

1948   September 19. The Baltimore Estonian Evangel-
                ical Lutheran Congregation was founded, with
                the Reverend Rudolf Troost as pastor. On Es-
                tonian Independence Day in 1969 (February 24)
                Troost gave the opening prayer in the House of
                Representatives. A second Estonian Lutheran
                congregation was established in March, 1951.
                Both have subparishes in Washington, D.C. The
                Baltimore congregation was the first one foun-
                ded by the postwar immigrants.

1949   Almost 400 Estonian displaced persons settled
                on the 19,000-acre Seabrook Farms in southern
                New Jersey, which specialized in the truck
                farming of vegetables. Most of the people had
                not engaged in agricultural pursuits before
                this, but they adjusted quickly to their new
                life. Initially, they moved into barracks

vacated by German prisoners of war who had
worked there. On July 31 the Seabrook Estonian Society was established with Albert
Vilms elected chairman. The founding of an
Estonian Lutheran congregation followed soon
thereafter, and an abandoned church was purchased for its use. In 1974, although many
Estonians had left Seabrook, the congregation
still numbered 200. A choir, boy and girl
scout units, and an Estonian-language Supplementary School were added in rapid succession.
Over the years, many in the group, especially
the young, left to pursue life elsewhere. In
1974 the Seabrook Farms Estonian-American
community celebrated its twenty-fifth anniversary, and the New Jersey state legislature
adopted a special resolution on the occasion.
(See Document No. 18.)

May. A Miami Estonian-American Cultural Club
was established with Julie Sööder elected
chairwoman. Later, the 100 household-strong
Miami Estonian-American community procured an
Estonian House for the club's use.

May. The first boy scout unit in the Estonian-American scouting movement was organized
in Seabrook, New Jersey, by Elmar Saarniit.
In the autumn of the same year an explorer
post was formed in New York City by Ilmar
Pleer. Massive organization got underway
with the founding of Boy Scout Troop 341 in
New York City in 1951. The movement has also
conducted periodic training camps for scout
leaders, most organized by Herbert Michelson,
who for many years was in charge of the Boy
Scouts of America Breyer Training Area near
Philadelphia. An international Estonian Boy
Scouts Association in Exile had been organized in West Germany and chartered in August,
1949, in London. The American-Estonian girl
scout movement was launched in 1949 with the
organization of two troops.

June 11. The first issue of a new Estonian-
language weekly newspaper, Vaba Eesti Sõna
(The Free Estonian Word), appeared in New
York with August Waldman as executive editor.
In 1974 the newspaper's circulation was 4,000.
Its senior editors are Erich Ernits and
Harald Raudsepp. Paul Saar is chairman of
the board. The newspaper has come to reflect
the dominant views of the older generation in

the second political wave of Estonian immigration to the United States -- the displaced
persons of World War Two. Most of them experienced Soviet rule in Estonia in 1940-1941
and fled westward in 1944 when Soviet armies
were about to again overrun Estonia. The
newspaper has been consequently strongly na-
tionalistic and staunchly anticommunist.

Summer. The first Estonian-American scout
camp was held on the property of an Estonian
poultry-farmer near Lakewood, New Jersey. For
several years thereafter an annual camp was
held on the lakeside property of another Estonian in the area. In 1956 a newly organized scouting booster organization purchased
a large plot of land in Jackson Township,
next to Lakewood, which was developed into a
permanent Estonian Scouting Reservation.

August. A permanent San Francisco Estonian
Society was established. Within a few years
it had grown to about 200 members and began
to publish its own quarterly, Sōnumid (Dis-
patches). In 1974 the society began serious-
ly to pursue plans to purchase an Estonian
House. Together with Estonian groups in Los
Angeles, Portland, Seattle and Vancouver, San
Francisco Estonian-Americans have organized
periodic West Coast Estonian Festivals. The
societies representing these five communities
are joined in an Estonian League of the West
Coast.

Fall. The New York Parish of the Estonian
Greek Orthodox Church was established with
the Very Reverend Aleksander Jürisson as
priest. In 1974 the parish had 200 members
and its services were conducted by the Very
Reverend Emmanuel Lepik from Toronto. There
are three other Estonian Orthodox parishes
in the United States: in Los Angeles, San
Francisco and Chicago.

THE 1950s: RAPID ORGANIZATIONAL GROWTH

1950   The 1950 census showed that there were a total of 10,085 persons born in Estonia living
in the United States. Gustav Härm, in an
article in the New York Estonian monthly Meie
Tee in 1967 reported that of this number
3,575 lived in New York State, 1,010 in New

Jersey, and 895 in California, with no other state having over 500. (See Table 4 in the Appendix.)

The Estonian Society of Buffalo was established under the chairmanship of Richard Valdov. Over the years its membership has ranged between 70 and 100, although there are about 350 Estonians in the area. The year 1952 saw the establishment of an Estonian Lutheran congregation and a mixed choir. Other activities sponsored by the society have included scouting and folkdancing. An Estonian-language Supplementary School was founded in 1961.

The operations of the Baltic Women's Council were transferred from West Germany, where it was organized in 1947, to New York City. The council has been very active in organizing social, cultural and youth activities, and in bringing to the world's attention the plight of the Baltic people under Soviet rule. Its members have actively participated in the life of American women's clubs and on the international scene. Among Estonian leaders in the council has been Mall Jürma. There are women's clubs in a number of Estonian-American centers in the United States, which together form the League of Estonian Women's Clubs, headquartered in New York City. An active leader in the Estonian women's clubs movement has been Juta Kurman. The first Estonian Women's Day in the United States was held in Seabrook, New Jersey, on March 5, 1950, with 65 participants.

January. A New York Estonian Theater was re-established under the leadership of Henrik Visnapuu. A renowned poet in his native land, Visnapuu arrived in the United States as a displaced person. Death put an end to his creative career at the age of 61 on April 3, 1951. The community established a literary fund in his name.

January 4. Estonian-Americans in the Albany-Schenectady (New York) area founded the Albany-Schenectady Estonian Association, with Peeter Kitzberg as chairman. About 200 Estonians were reported to be in the area.

January 8. An Estonian Students Association
in the United States was established in New
York, with Peeter Elias elected chairman. Very
active in its early years in political, cultural and social activities, in recent years
the association's major emphasis has been on
organizing skiing weekends for young Estonian-
Americans.

May 5. Plans were formulated for a second Estonian relief organization. By early July its
name was affixed as Eesti Abi (Estonian Aid),
and it was incorporated in New York State. Its
major purpose was to assist Estonian refugees
still in Europe, to lobby for Estonian interests in regard to American immigration laws,
to provide opportunities for Estonian children
in America to spend their summers outside the
cities, and to assist Estonian-American college students financially. The organization's
first president was the distinguished Estonian
diplomat, Kaarel R. Pusta. In its twentieth
anniversary report in 1970, Estonian Aid noted
that it had provided more than $200,000 in
general assistance, and large additional sums
for specific projects. Contributions are sol-
icited from the Estonian-American community,
but significant sums have been donated by the
William Zimdin Foundation and Catholic Relief
Services.

June. Ten-year old Jaan Äärismaa won first
prize in the New York Daily News art-drawing
contest for children. Young Äärismaa arrived
in the United States only a month before the
contest. His prize was a cowboy outfit. Äärismaa later became a top illustrator for one
of the largest New York department stores.

August 12. An Estonian Philatelic Society was
founded in New York with A. Vahter elected
president. Since 1953 the office has been
held by A.E. Pensa. In 1955 the organization
began to issue the periodical Eesti Filatelist
(Estonian Philatelist) under Pensa's editorship. After ten issues, its publication was
transferred to Sweden. In 1972 the society
began to publish its own Bulletään (Bulletin),
under the editorship of Rudolf Hämar. By
1965 the association had 145 members and 27
corresponding members, many of whom have won
prizes at international exhibitions.

December 16. The Estonian Learned Society in
America was formed by Estonian scholars who
had settled in the United States after World
War Two, with Dr. Nikolai Maim as the first
president. Operating initially under the auspices of the New York Estonian Educational Society, it subsequently became an independent
organization. Its primary aim has been the
advancement of Estonian studies through lectures, publications and financial support. In
1954 an English-language Yearbook was published, and four subsequent volumes have appeared at irregular intervals. The Yearbooks
contain articles by society members on a wide
variety of topics. The society has also published the following works: Estonian Poetry
and Language: Essays in Honor of Ants Oras
(edited by Viktor Kõressaar and Aleksis Rannit, 1965), Mundology or World Science (by
Nikolai Maim, 1966), Literatures in Contact:
Finland and Estonia (by George Kurman, 1972),
and A Bibliography of English-Language Sources
on Estonia: Periodicals, Pamphlets and Books
(compiled by Marju Rink Parming and Tõnu Parming, 1974). A translation of the Roman author Vergil's Bucolica from Latin to Estonian
by Ants Oras was issued in 1970. Regular membership in the society has been restricted to
individuals with degrees at the master or doctoral level. The Estonian Learned Society in
America at the end of 1974 had 200 members,
most of whom had received their highest degree
from an American college or university. The
society's officers during its twenty-fifth
year of existence in 1975 are: Viktor Kõressaar, president; Tõnu Parming, secretary; and
Villi Kangro, treasurer.

1951   March 4. William Zimdin, Estonian-born mil-
lionaire, died. Born in 1881, Zimdin had extensive holdings in this country and abroad.
When he first arrived in the United States in
1920, he got his start by arranging business
deals between America and Soviet Russia. He
settled permanently in the United States in
1940. He bequeathed one million dollars to
help refugees from communism, and he also contributed to Estonian charities.

March 8. The first Estonian-American boy
scout meeting in New York City was held with
six boys and one scoutmaster in attendance.
The troop, better known by its name, Viiking

(Viking), was not the oldest in the United
States (there were two slightly older ones,
including an explorer post founded in New
York the previous year), but it quickly grew
into the largest. By the end of the year
Viiking had 45 members, and by 1956, 105. Its
leadership has almost always been in the hands
of three able scoutmasters: Linold Milles,
Harry Tarmo and Erni Kilm. For a time, Viiking published its own magazine by the same
name, edited by various young members. The
unit is still active presently. Several cub
scouts are the sons of early members.

Estonian boy scout units in America have
always been affiliated with the Boy Scouts of
America. At the end of 1974 there were 185
Estonian boy scouts and 53 leaders in 10 units,
centralized under the Estonian Boy Scout Council in America, headed by Mati Kōiva of Connecticut.

1952   Korean War. Kalju Suitsev, who was severely
wounded in 1951 in Wonju, was awarded a Silver Star, a Purple Heart and other medals for
bravery. During an earlier engagement he had
virtually singlehandedly held his company's
position by killing 37 North Koreans attacking
it. When his own ammunition ran out, he
grabbed weapons from fallen comrades and continued firing. Suitsev was born in Estonia
in 1930. Several other Estonian immigrants
died in the conflict.

May. More than 4,000 Estonians in the United
States elected delegates to a Representative
Assembly of the newly-formed Estonian National
Committee in the United States. A charter was
ratified in July and the organization began to
function by the fall. According to its charter, the committee was to work towards the
restoration of Estonian independence; to struggle against communism and other forms of to-
talitarianism; to preserve Estonian national
culture in exile; to help Estonians adjust to
the American way of life; to support civil
rights and to further a democratic world out-
look.

The Estonian National Committee, with its
Canadian counterpart, has also organized Estonian folk festivals in North America. These
events have drawn over 5,000 participants in
New York and Toronto. Finally, the committee
has organized periodic Congresses of Estonian

Organizations in America. The first president of the Estonian National Committee was Professor Juhan Vasar (1952-1956). The following have held the office afterward: August Kärsna (1956-1959); Julius Kangur (1959-1964); Heikki Leesment (1964-1971); and Ilmar Pleer (1971 to date). In 1972 the committee changed its name to Estonian American National Council.

1953   May. Estonian male choruses in North America converged on Toronto for the first Meeslaulupäevad (Male Chorus Days). The event has subsequently alternated between Toronto and New York (or Lakewood, New Jersey). The tenth Male Chorus Days were held in 1974, again in Canada. Similar periodic events for female choruses began in 1954.

1954   The First Synod of the Estonian Evangelical Lutheran Church began functioning under Reverend Aleksander Hinno. Congregations subject to its jurisdiction were located in Baltimore, Buffalo, Cleveland, Connecticut, Lakewood (New Jersey), Los Angeles, New York and Albany-Schenectady. A second Synod began operations under Reverend Valter Viks, with congregations located in Detroit, Portland,Minneapolis, San Francisco, Seattle, New York (Lexington Avenue), Washington-Baltimore and Chicago. Estonian Lutheran Synods have come into being in several Western countries since 1944, and they are united under the Estonian Evangelical Lutheran Church, which presently is headquartered in exile in Stockholm, Sweden, with the Reverend Konrad Veem as archbishop. In 1968 the First Synod had 13 congregations with 4,700 members, served by 10 pastors. The synod in 1968 began publishing a religious periodical, Oma Kirik (Our Own Church).

A pamphlet entitled New Yorgi Eesti Haridusselts 1954 (The New York Estonian Educational Society in 1954), edited by its secretary, Bernhard Parming, noted that substantial progress had been made in constructing a children's camp on Long Island. About ten acres had been purchased under the leadership of Feliks Simmerman a few years earlier in Middle Island, in a location known for some time as "Estonian village" because many Estonian-American families resided there.

Through the voluntary contributions of money, labor and materials, the New York Estonian Educational Society erected a large, modern building and several cabins to be used as an Estonian children's camp. A swimming pool was added at the end of the decade. For almost two decades the camp has served Estonian children throughout the country. Although the six-week summer camps have been primarily recreational, Estonian folk dances, folk songs, and at times even language have been taught and emphasized. A long-time camp leader was Henn Hendriksson. The facility has been used also for other activities, such as athletic events, folk festivals and so forth, and a few years ago a memorial was erected to Estonian war veterans. For a number of years during the 1950s and 1960s the main building housed a local elementary school during the winters.

January 22. Concert violinist Evi Liivak received good reviews for her American debut at New York's Town Hall. Liivak, who graduated from the Tallinn Conservatory in 1939 at the age of 14, married an American concert pianist, Richard Anschütz, in 1950 and came to the United States the following year. She has also studied in Budapest, Berlin, and Paris and has appeared in concert with many European symphony orchestras. She is still currently active.

1955 Government statistics on immigration and naturalization for 1935 and 1955 indicated that Estonians were acquiring American citizenship faster than almost any other group of immigrants. (See Table 2 in the Appendix.)

Olev Träss graduated from Princeton University as valedictorian, the first such distinction by a young Estonian at a leading American university. Subsequently, he received a Ph.D. in chemical engineering from Massachusetts Institute of Technology. Träss has been on the faculty of the University of Toronto since then.

The first Estonian Kentucky Colonel was probably Dr. Eugene Püss. A graduate of the University of Tartu Medical School in Estonia, Püss came to Kentucky after World War Two. He first worked as a doctor in residence and

subsequently as deputy director of the Tuber-
culosis Hospital in Glasgow, Kentucky, for
which he received a governor's appointment as
a Kentucky Colonel.

October 1. A new world-wide Estonian organization founded in New York the previous year
held its first meeting there with Dr. Juhan
Vasar as chairman. The Ülemaailmne Eesti
Kesknōukogu (The Estonian World Council) has
represented central Estonian organizations in
a number of Western countries through delegates in the United States. Its principal
aim from the outset was the coordination of
efforts to liberate Estonia from Soviet rule.
It has sent out numerous memorandums, position papers and pamphlets in several languages to governments and appropriate organizations. One of its most important efforts
was related to the European Security and Cooperation Conference of 1973 and 1974 in Hel-
sinki and Geneva. The council sent observers
and activists to the sites of the conference
to insure that it not accord diplomatic recognition to the Soviet annexation of Estonia.
This effort was, furthermore, coordinated
with Latvian and Lithuanian organizations.
(See Document No. 13.)

1956   Estonian-born artist Alexander Yaron's por-
            trait of Mamie Eisenhower was presented to
            her by the New York Eisenhower-Nixon Commit-
            tee on the occasion of her sixtieth birthday.

            May 7. The Federation of Associations for the
            Advancement of Estonian Youth was incorporated
            in New Jersey. Essentially a booster organi-
            zation for Estonian scouting in America, the
            federation was formed on December 27, 1953.
            By 1967 the organization had an operating
            budget of over $45,000. The federation's ma-
            jor achievement was the purchase of eighty-
            two acres of land in Jackson, New Jersey, in
            1956, which was developed into a permanent
            Estonian Scouting Reservation in the United
            States. In addition to annual scouting camps
            during the summers since then, the reservation
            hosted a world-wide Estonian scout jamboree
            in 1967. By this time the federation had
            erected a number of large buildings on the
            reservation. Construction and development of
            the site was from the outset based on the do-
            nation of labor, money, machines and materials

by Estonian-Americans, foremost by members
of the nearby Lakewood Estonian Association.
In addition to scouting activities, the site
has been used frequently during the summer
months by other Estonian organizations on
the East Coast for their get-togethers. Individuals active in the leadership of the federation have included Aleksander Prima, Val-
fried Gutman, Parfeni Valgemäe, Marta Lannus,
Henno Keerdoja, Heikki Leesment, Meta Mäekask,
Olev Piirsalu, Harry Verder, and Ernst Luebik.
At present the reservation is threatened by
the construction of a major highway through
the middle of it.

July 19. A number of people interested in
Estonian music formed an appropriate centralized organization, the Eesti Helikunsti Keskus (The Estonian Music Center), in New York,
with August Ruut as the first chairman. Afterward, the center's activities have been
largely overseen by its present chairwoman,
Juta Kurman. The purpose of the center has
been to assist the continued creative development of Estonian music outside Estonia
and to introduce Estonian music to the American public. These objectives have been met
through the organization of recitals and concerts, the collection and publication of
sheet music, and the award of scholarships to
Estonian-American youth studying music. Concerts by Estonian composers, instrumentalists
and vocalists, who often are brought to the
United States from Europe and Canada for this
purpose, have been sponsored in leading reci-
tal halls. The center recently announced the
establishment of an Estonian Music Archives
in the United States.

1957   The Foundation for Estonian Arts and Letters
(Eesti Kultuurfond) was founded in New York
City. Incorporated in 1965, the foundation's
purpose was "to promote understanding and
knowledge of arts, science, literature and
Estonian language...to arrange literary programs...to hold competitions and exhibitions
...to extend financial aid." Individuals who
have been especially active in the foundation's activities include Karl Jõgise, Viktor
Kõressaar and Villi Kangro. The foundation
has been one of the primary sponsors of Estonian cultural life in America. It has organized various lectures, symposia, conferences,

exhibits and recitals. One of its most important recent activities has been the establishment of a collection of Estonian art. International in scope, the founders of the
collection hope to expand it to the point
where it would become a Museum of Estonian
Art outside of Estonia. Additionally, the
foundation has supported the publication of
various works and supported the construction
of the Estonian Archives in the United States
in Lakewood, New Jersey.

Estonian youth in the Midwest, led by Reet
Ülper and Enn Arike, decided to form the
Kesk-Lääne Eesti Noorte Koondis (The Midwest
Estonian Youth Association), with an avowed
purpose of providing a social and cultural
outlet for youth in the region. The association has sponsored annual "Friendship Days,"
which have rotated between various midwestern
cities, from Minneapolis to Columbus, Ohio.
These have been both social events and cultural symposiums, with Estonian scholars contributing appropriate lectures.

Mihkel Viise became the first Estonian "flying pastor," a chaplain in the United States
Air Force, with the rank of first lieutenant.
His father was a pastor and his brother a pilot who died in a crash some years ago. By
1969 Viise had attained the rank of lieutenant colonel and was assigned to Air Force
units in Germany.

Aleksander Aspel, who promoted French culture
in prewar Estonia, was now doing the same in
the United States by coediting (with the American poet Paul Engle) a book commemorating
the 100th anniversary of Baudelaire's Fleurs
du mal. Aspel has also authored works such
as Textbook of French Literary Recordings
(Part I in 1954 and Part II in 1958) and
Contemporary French Poetry (1965). Aspel,
born in 1908, studied Romance languages and
literature at the University of Tartu in Estonia and subsequently at the Sorbonne in
Paris. He arrived in the United States in
1946, joining the faculty of Iowa State University, where he was appointed full professor and chairman of the Romance Languages Department in 1954.

January 20. Ludvig Juht, contrabass soloist
with the Boston Symphony, died. Born in Estonia in 1894, Juht took up playing the trum-
pet, flute and trombone in his village orchestra at the age of seven. By fourteen he had
switched to the contrabass. After taking some
lessons, he began to play in town orchestras
in Estonia and Finland. He continued playing
and pursued further study in Berlin, giving
his first solo concert there in 1922. In 1927
he returned to his native country and for
three years worked for the Estonia Opera and
the Symphony Orchestra in Tallinn. London and
Riga followed thereafter, and by 1934 Juht was
engaged by Serge Koussevitzky as first contrabass soloist with the Boston Symphony. He remained in that position until his death, although he went on individual concert tours as
well. Since 1945 he was also with the Music
Department of Boston University, and from 1946,
with the New England Conservatory. Juht's
contrabass solos were considered remarkable
because he handled the instrument as if it
were a violincello, the scores of which he actually used. He also wrote compositions for
the contrabass. Juht was very active in Estonian-American social life and was one of
the founding members of the Boston Estonian
Society in 1936. His initiative also helped
establish the World Association of Estonians.
In addition, Juht wrote for Estonian-language
publications. On his concert tours, he never
failed to include at least one piece by an Estonian composer. Dr. Charles Munch, conductor
of the Boston Symphony Orchestra at the time
that Juht died, had the following comment:
"Juht was not only a great artist but also a
great patriot."

May. Thousands of Estonians from the United
States and Canada gathered in Toronto for the
First North American Estonian Festival. Cultural events and exhibits, performances by
folk dancers, gymnasts and choruses were in
the schedule, as well as social events. The
patrons of the festival were the prime minister of Ontario Province and the mayor of Toronto. The Reverend Aleksander Abel of Connecticut was a festival vice-president. Subsequently, the festival has alternated between
New York (1960 and 1967) and Toronto (1964).
These two cities along with Stockholm, Sweden,
have been the largest sites of Estonian set-

tlement outside of Estonia.

1958   October 27. Artist Andrew [Andres] George
Winter died. Winter, born in Estonia in 1893,
was a seaman before he arrived in the United
States. A citizen since 1921, he studied at
the National Academy of Design in New York
and subsequently in Rome and Paris. In 1938
he was elected a National Academician by the
National Academy of Arts. After a sojourn in
the Virgin Islands, Winter and his American-
born wife, Mary Taylor-Winter, settled on Mon-
hegan Island off the coast of Maine. His
paintings are realistic, depicting the sea and
seafaring, such as his sketches of the Coast
Guard cutter Champlain. He was also well-known
for his winter scenes ("Winter is his name and
his season"). In 1950 The Christian Science
Monitor featured a new painting, A September
Afternoon. Winter's works are found in muse-
ums and in private collections such as those
of the Edisons, Vanderbilts and Chamberlains.

1959   May. Professor Ragnar Nurkse, born in Estonia in 1907, died in Vevey, Switzerland, where
he was vacationing. Nurkse was professor of
economics at Columbia University. The university subsequently honored him by establishing
a Ragnar Nurkse Chair in Economics. Nurkse
authored numerous studies, the most important
being International Currency Experience (1944)
and Problems of Capital Formation in Underde-
veloped Countries (1953). He studied economics at Tartu University and subsequently at
Edinburgh University, Vienna and Geneva. In
1934 he joined the staff of the League of Nations. During World War Two he continued in
this capacity in the United States, until
joining the faculty of Columbia University in
1945 where he became a full professor in 1947.

August. The ninety-man New York Estonian Male
Chorus was ten years old. Directed initially
by Manivald Loite, the choir has performed on
the New York concert stage and at the White
House, and has gone on foreign tours all the
way to Finland. In 1975, members of the chorus, together with singers from Canada, plan
to fly to Australia to give several concerts
there. For a number of years the chorus had
a female director, Maaja Duesberg, who received her professional education in the United States after World War Two.

October. An extensive statistical survey of
Estonian youth in America was presented by
Karl Urm to the Congress of Estonian Organizations in New York. Conducted during the
preceding two years, it covered 425 youth in
Estonian Supplementary Schools. Among the interesting findings were that 70.6 percent of
the families had working mothers; 75 percent
had a television set; 69 percent had a car;
40 percent had a piano; and 38 percent lived
in their own homes. A high 97.6 percent of
the families purchased Estonian-language
books. In 67.3 percent of the homes only Estonian was spoken; in a mere 0.7 percent was
English the only language used. However, Urm
found that when the youngsters were with sib-
lings or peers, only 16 percent used Estonian
alone; 82 percent used Estonian and English
intermittently. Of the boys, 51 percent be-
longed to an Estonian scout unit, as did 45
percent of the girls. However, 31 percent of
the boys and 37 percent of the girls were not
members of any Estonian youth organization
other than the supplementary school.

In concluding the statistical analysis
of the data, Urm expressed dissatisfaction
with what the group was doing to preserve an
Estonian identity among its youth. He stated:
"There is a very deep and receptive interest
among our youth for things Estonian; that the
youngsters' actual knowledge of Estonia is
extremely limited, and that their ability in
the Estonian language is deficient in spite
of this interest, this is a matter for which
we should blame ourselves -- parents, Estonian societies, and the ethnic group as a
whole."

THE 1960s: STABILIZATION AND ASSIMILATION

1960   The United States census indicated that there
were 19,938 first and second generation Estonians in the country. These figures did not,
of course, include subsequent generations of
Estonian ancestry nor ethnic Estonians who
were born in countries other than Estonia.
Of this number, 6,002 lived in New York
State, 2,572 in California, 2,071 in New
Jersey, and 1,000 in Connecticut. Almost
half of the group lived in the corridor from
Washington, D.C., to Boston. Another 19 percent lived in the states around the Great

Lakes, from Ohio to Wisconsin, and 17 percent
on the West Coast. The overwhelming majority
were in urban areas. (See Table 4 in the Appendix.)

A specialist on Milton, Shelley and T.S.
Eliot, and with more than 100 articles in five
languages to his credit, Professor Ants Oras
saw the publication of his latest work this
year, "Pause Patterns in Elizabethan and Ja-
cobean Drama," as he turned sixty. Born in
Tallinn, Oras studied at Tartu, Leipzig and
Oxford Universities. In 1932 he was appointed a professor of English at Tartu University.
As a refugee in Sweden during World War Two,
Oras worked for the United States Embassy in
Stockholm. After the war he proceeded to Cambridge University and then to the Bodleyan Library at Oxford University. During that time
he was active in reinstituting the Estonian
Centre of the International P.E.N. Club. In
1949 he became full professor of English at
the University of Florida, Gainesville. As a
professor emeritus he was honored, in 1972,
by his students and was given a special prize
for his scholarly work.

1961   Aleksis Rannit was appointed curator of Slavic
and East European studies at Yale University.
Rannit, born in Estonia in 1914, is a poet,
critic and essayist of international reputa-
tion and his poems have appeared in several
languages. His first collection of poetry
was published in 1937 in Estonia. He arrived
in the United States in 1953. In 1968 Yale
University organized a Symposium on Estonian
Poetry under Rannit's leadership. In November,
1974, the Yale Library Associates organized
a reading of Rannit's poetry. Poems were presented in Estonian, English, Spanish, Chinese,
German and Russian by seven readers, preceded
by an introduction by the distinguished scholar Norman H. Pearson. For two months the university's Sterling Memorial Library had a special display of Rannit's poetry and the works
of the Estonian artist Eduard Wiiralt. Rannit's poetry has appeared in English translation by Henry Lyman in New Directions, Volume
25, 1972.

March. Dr. Otto G. Lellep, a metallurgical
engineer, was given the Milwaukee International Institute's Distinguished Service Award.

In 1959 Lellep had received a gold medal in
West Germany for his contributions to the use
of oxygen in steel processing. Lellep, born
in Estonia in 1884, arrived in the United
States in 1917. Between the two world wars,
Lellep worked in Germany as an American citizen and developed new cement baking ovens,
manufactured under the trade name "Lepol."
Lellep returned to the United States in 1940
and soon went into partnership with the Allis
Chalmers Company to produce these ovens for
the Western hemisphere. His inventions have
also had an impact on the production of nick-
el and iron ore. Lellep has contributed a
substantial amount of money to support Estonian youth activities in the United States
through a trust fund.

May 1. The Estonian Students Fund was incorporated with the aim of promoting Estonian
studies and assisting Estonian-American students. The idea for creating such an organization originated among student activists in
New York during the 1950s. The incorporation
documents were signed by the following five
individuals, all of whom have remained prominent in the fund's activities: Rudolf Hämar,
Helmo Raag, Virko Keder, William Salmre, and
Vootele Vaska. The present president of the
fund is Kadri Niider.
     Two aspects of the fund's activities merit
special attention. One of its first programs
was the establishment of a scholarship for
sending Estonian-Americans to study at Finnish
universities. To date 28 individuals have
used the opportunity to pursue postgraduate
studies in Finland, the country which is cul-
turally and linguistically closest to Estonia.
Almost all of the scholarship recipients have
to some degree pursued the study of the Estonian language while in Finland. In conjunction with this program, the fund has organized
Finnish-Estonian cultural and social gatherings in New York. Financially, a more encompassing program has been the award of scholarships to Estonian-American undergraduate and
graduate students in the United States. To
date the fund has awarded more than $100,000
in various scholarships. Almost all of the
money represents contributions from within
the Estonian-American community. A major
share represents interest income from a special trust established by Otto G. Lellep in

memory of his father. A trust established
by Aleksander Kütt also provides scholarship
funds.

1962   A survey indicated that Estonian academic organizations (fraternities, sororities, and associations) in exile admitted 529 new members
between 1946 and 1962, most of whom were born
between 1927 and 1944. Their fields of study
were: sciences -- 18 percent; engineering and
other applied fields -- 43 percent; humanities -- 16 percent; social sciences -- 16
percent; and health and medicine -- 7 percent.
While not all Estonian youth studying at
American universities joined the exiled student organizations, the above choice of fields
of study probably indicated a general trend.

Agate Veeber's Angel I was selected by the
Society of American Graphic Artists for a
tour of South America, the Far East and Af-
rica along with other American artists. Her
works have been acquired by the Metropolitan
Museum of Art, the New York Public Library
Print Collection, the Cincinnati Museum of
Art and the Albright Art Gallery in Buffalo.
Veeber is a graduate of the Pallas School of
Art in Estonia.

The American Volleyball Association gave Dr.
Martin Mägi the title of "All-American 1962."
The young Estonian-born doctor was the cap-
tain of the Alameda Naval Air Station team.
He received the same title again in 1963.

Narda Onyx [Gladys Viirand], who has appeared
in numerous TV dramatizations and also in the
movies, joined the cast of the "Beverly Hill-
billies." Her first TV appearance was in "A
Ticket for Thaddeus" with Edmund O'Brien in
1955. Onyx fled Estonia during the war and
began her stage career in England, where she
was "discovered" by Sir Laurence Olivier.
She moved to southern California in 1954 by
way of Canada.

May. Edmund Valtman [Vallot], a political
cartoonist for The Hartford Times in Connecticut, received the 1961 Pulitzer Prize for
the best cartoon of the year (depicting Cu-
ba's Castro). Valtman, born in Estonia in
1914, came to the United States in 1949.
President Johnson obtained 50 Valtman origi-

nals. They are now at the Johnson Library in
Austin, Texas. A collection of more than 300
Valtman cartoons is at Wichita State Univer-
sity in Kansas.

June. Estonian-born John Part was elected
Shrimp King at the Shrimp Festival in Browns-
ville, Texas. A number of enterprising Estonians took to shrimping in the late 1940s,
first in Florida and subsequently in Texas.
None had been shrimpers before and some had
not even fished. The only requirement was,
as one of them put it, that "the person, who
wishes to become a shrimp fisherman must first
of all be immune to sea-sickness." By the
1970s the Estonian-owned shrimp fleet in Texas
had grown to more than twenty-five boats owned
by some half a dozen Estonians, seven by a
company called "Estotex."

1963   Elmar Leppik, a biologist at Iowa State Uni-
            versity, was elected by the 1962-1963 Commit-
            tee on Who is Who in American Education to
            membership in Leaders of American Science.
            He has subsequently received similar recogni
            tion from other organizations both in the
            United States and internationally. A scien-
            tist with about 375 publications to his cred-
            it, Leppik graduated from the University of
            Tartu in Estonia and received a doctoral de-
            gree from Zürich Technical University in
            Switzerland. He arrived in the United States
            in 1950 and at first was on the faculty of
            Augustana College (Sioux Falls, South Dakota)
            and the University of Minnesota. For the last
            ten years Leppik has been a research scientist
            at the Plant Genetics and Germ Plasm Institute
            of the Beltsville Agricultural Research Center,
            United States Department of Agriculture, in
            Maryland. A specialist in the areas of bee
            behavior, floral evolution and the gene cen-
            ters of cultivated plants, Leppik has been a
            fellow of the Rockefeller Foundation. Addi-
            tionally, he has done research at the Tropi-
            cal Research Institute in El Salvador.

1964-   Viet Nam War. A large number of Estonian
1972   youth, both as volunteers and draftees, par-
            ticipated in the Viet Nam conflict. One of
            the first Estonian-American fatalities in the
            war, in 1966, was Air Force Lieutenant Aavo
            Komendant of Lakewood, New Jersey, when the
            aircraft he piloted was shot down. He was

missing in action and later declared dead.
Army Lieutenant Mark N. Enari was killed in
action in the same year, while saving his
unit from ambush by manning a machinegun. He
was posthumously awarded the Silver Star for
valor and the Fourth Infantry Division base
camp near Pleiku was named for him (Camp Enari).

The following year saw the death of in-
fantryman Jaak Kuri of Washington, D.C., the
point man on an ambushed patrol. Kuri was
posthumously awarded several decorations. In
1969 Specialist Fourth Class Lauri Kangro of
New York City died in battle, and was posthumously awarded several decorations for val-
or. 1970 saw the death of Endel Palgi of
Fayetteville, North Carolina, a retired Army
sergeant major who was a civilian advisor.
Palgi had arrived in the United States just
prior to World War Two, and he began his military career in that conflict. He was a very
highly decorated soldier, having served in
World War Two, in the Korean War, and afterward in Laos and several times in Viet Nam.
Palgi, like a number of Estonian-American officers and enlisted men, was a member of the
Army's elite Special Forces, the "Green Be-
rets." Finally, 1971 saw the death of Corpo-
ral Toivo D. Nõmm of Baltimore.

Several additional Estonian-Americans who
distinguished themselves were Major Jüri
Toomepuu, an Army helicopter pilot, who was
awarded the nation's second highest medal for
valor, the Distinguished Service Cross; Captain Hans Tees, wounded four times in ten
months, who was awarded a Silver Star and
Bronze Star for valor in saving and inspiring
his injured troops under fire; and Sergeant
First Class Harry Isak, who received several
Bronze Stars for valor for carrying out wounded under fire and for taking command of his
unit after the officers were killed or wounded.

1964   Two more Estonian Houses were acquired by Estonian societies, one in Baltimore and the
other in Minneapolis. This made for a total
of seven in the United States. The others
were in New York, Seabrook (New Jersey),
Lakewood (New Jersey), Miami and Los Angeles.
Estonian Houses were subsequently also established in Chicago and San Francisco. The
Baltimore Estonian House in September, 1974,

celebrated its tenth anniversary. It is now
under the leadership of Peeter Kiik, a Baltimore architect, who came to the United States
as a small child after World War Two and grew
up in the city. (See Document No. 19.)

Dr. Igor Tamm was appointed professor and
senior physician at Rockefeller University in
New York. Tamm, born in Estonia in 1922, arrived in the United States in 1945 and joined
the research staff of the university in 1949.
He has specialized in viral replication and
virus-induced alterations in cells, biosyn-
thesis of nucleic acids and proteins, and in
the interaction of viruses with mucoproteins.
Tamm was also a consultant to the Sloan-Ket-
tering Institute of Cancer Research.

June 21. Construction of an Estonian Lutheran church in Lakewood, New Jersey, was nearly
complete, and the congregation held its first
official service in its new home. The church
was the second one erected by Estonian immigrants in the United States, the first having
been at Gleason, Wisconsin, in 1914. The
church was constructed largely through the
donation of money, labor and materials by the
local Estonian-American community. Several
hundred people contributed to the project.
The largest financial contributor was Leopold
Haus ($931.50); the largest contributor of
materials was the Harry Must Company
($1925.80); and Robert Kasenurm was the lar-
gest individual contributor of labor (485
hours). The Estonian Evangelical Lutheran
Congregation of the Holy Ghost in 1964 had
402 members.

1965   Between July, 1940, and June, 1965, a total
of 14,017 Estonian immigrants entered the
United States. From 1923 to 1939 about 2,900
had entered the country. (See Table 1 in the
Appendix.)

Having appeared in Sweden since 1957, the
publication of Mana, an international review
of Estonian literature, art and science, was
transferred to the United States. To date
sixteen issues have been published here under
the editorship of Hellar Grabbi. Mana contains scholarly articles, commentary and re-

views on all aspects of Estonian culture, and
additionally features original fiction and poetry, as well as translation of non-Estonian
poetry into Estonian. Although the contents
are in Estonian, the journal contains English
summaries. A product of the younger generation of Estonian scholars and cultural activists residing in the West, Mana has represented the avant garde in Estonian culture world-
wide.

March. John Kusik [Johannes Kuusik], born in
Estonia in 1898, became director and senior
vice president of the Baltimore and Ohio Railroad. He also was appointed board member of
the Cleveland Electric Illuminating Company,
replacing Cyrus S. Eaton. In 1966 he was
named, additionally, vice chairman of the
Chesapeake and Ohio Railway. Kusik holds a
Master of Science degree from the University
of Virginia (1925). He was awarded an honorary Doctor of Engineering degree by Case Institute of Technology in 1955.

Christmas. Artist Karl Pehme designed the
Christmas display at Rockefeller Center, New
York City. Pehme, born in 1918, studied
sculpture at the National School of Higher
Art in Estonia and after the war in Paris.
He came to America in 1952 and began working
as a professional artist. His display at
Rockefeller Center was repeated for several
years. Pehme was also responsible for a
Christmas display at the city's Pan-Am Build-
ing.

1966   Louvain University in Belgium published Dr.
Arthur Võõbus' 400-page History of the School
of Nisibis, based on original sources which
he discovered during research in the Middle
East. Võõbus, born in 1909, obtained his doctorate at the University of Tartu in Estonia
in 1943, immigrating to the United States after the war. Since 1948 he has been a professor at the Lutheran School of Theology at
Chicago. A biblical scholar, specialist in
early Christianity, and the world's leading
Syriologist, Võõbus has published over 47
books and 300 articles in several languages.
These have included, for example: Early Ver-
sions of the New Testament (1954), the two-
volume History of Asceticism in the Syrian
Orient (1962), and Discovery of Very Impor-

tant Manuscript Sources for the Syro-Roman
Lawbook (1973). Vööbus is also authoring a
multivolume English-language history of Estonia, the first three volumes of which have
been published: Studies in the History of
the Estonian People (1969, 1970, and 1974).
Lastly, Vööbus was instrumental in creating
the scholarly series, "Papers of the Estonian Theological Society in Exile" in which almost 30 volumes have been published. In early 1974 Dr. Vööbus was nominated and admitted
to membership in the Belgian Royal Academy of
Sciences, Letters and Arts. Earlier, he had
become a member of the International Society
of Sciences and Letters in Paris.

Taavo Virkhaus, who hails from a long line of
Estonian musicians, was awarded the Howard
Hansen Prize for his violin concerto. The
following year he obtained a Doctor of Musical Arts degree from the Eastman School at
the University of Rochester, where he has
been director of music, an associate professor, and conductor of the university's symphony orchestra since. He is also the music
director of the Opera Theater of Rochester.
Virkhaus was born in Estonia in 1934 and im-
migrated to the United States after World
War Two.

January. A survey conducted among 885 Estonians in Southern California -- 437 males
and 448 females, most of them residents of
Los Angeles County -- showed that every fifth
Estonian worked in the field of specializa-
tion which he or she had obtained in college.
Among the young, every second Estonian had or
was getting a university education. Divided
into 383 households, the survey showed, furthermore, that 36 households had an annual
income of $4,000 or less; 118 of $4,000 to
$7,000; 159 of $7,000 to $12,000; and 70 of
$12,000 or more. Two-hundred and thirty-
eight lived in their own homes.

February 12. The younger generation of Bal-
tic political activists founded a new organ-
ization, Baltic Appeal to the United Nations
(BATUN). An outgrowth of the Baltic Freedom
Rally of November, 1965, BATUN has been very
active in promoting the cause of freedom for
Estonia, Latvia and Lithuania at the United
Nations. Additionally, it has provided gen-

eral informational services and sponsored
cultural events. BATUN subsequently became
a department of the more encompassing United
Baltic Appeal, Inc. As BATUN before it, the
United Baltic Appeal is a non-partisan group
with a prime purpose of "working toward self-
determination for Estonia, Latvia and Lithuania." Estonian-Americans active in the two
organizations have been: Victor Vinkman,
Tõnu Espenberg, Karl Laantee, Heino Ainso,
Andres Jüriado, Mari Linnamaa, Juta Virkmaa
and Rein Virkmaa.

August. The 9th Coordinated International
Chemistry Congress announced a "Vaska compound," named after Dr. Lauri Vaska. The
compound opened up new areas of research in
homogeneous catalysis and oxygen-carrying
complexes. Vaska, born in Estonia in 1925,
has been a professor at the Clarkson College
of Technology at Potsdam, New York. He began
his studies in chemistry at Göttingen University in Germany and completed them at the
University of Texas in Austin. The compound
was the result of Vaska's research at the Mel-
lon Institute in Pittsburgh.

1967   Younger generation Estonian scholars and ac-
          tivists founded a cultural symposium, liter-
          ally, in the forest. Although conducted in
          Canada, many student participants and a very
          large share of the faculty have been drawn
          from the United States. Called Metsaülikool
          (University in the Forest), it has been held
          annually at the Estonian Scouting Reservation
          north of Toronto. In 1974 it was held in
          Finland. It has had about 150 annual parti-
          cipants, who include youth aged eighteen to
          thirty-five and Estonian scholars and cultur-
          al figures. Each session has been a ten-day
          saturated "Estonian consciousness-raising,"
          and it has become popular among college-age
          youth.

          Estonian girl scouts and boy scouts in the
          United States sponsored a world-wide jamboree
          of Estonian scouting, attracting youth from
          Australia to Sweden. The event, named Koguja
          (The Gatherer), was under the leadership of
          scoutmaster Linold Milles of New York City
          and was attended by over 1,000 scouts and
          their leaders. Subsequent world-wide jambo-
          rees have been held in West Germany (1970),

in Canada (1972) and in Sweden (1975). Estonian-American scouting units have participated in each.

The government of Finland awarded Professor
Jaan Puhvel an Order of the White Rose, First
Class, for his contributions to Fenno-Ugric
studies. Puhvel, born in 1932 in Estonia,
received his Ph.D. in philology from Harvard
University in 1959. He is director of the
Center of Language Studies and chairman of
the Department of Classics at the University
of California, Los Angeles.

Felix Oinas authored a textbook for teaching
Estonian to non-Estonians. A professor of
Slavic and Fenno-Ugric languages at Indiana
University and a fellow of the Folklore In-
stitute, Oinas was born in Estonia in 1911.
He received his initial higher education at
the Universities of Tartu, Budapest and
Heidelberg. Arriving in the United States
in 1950, he obtained a Ph.D. from Indiana
University. Oinas has been awarded numerous
distinguished grants such as those by the
Guggenheim Foundation (1966) and the National Endowment for the Humanities (1973) to
study folklore. He has also been a Fulbright
visiting professor at Finnish universities.
The Finnish Academy of Sciences has published
his monograph, Studies in Finnish-Slavic
Folklore Relations, and the Finnish government has honored him with a service medal.

Estonian Events, a bimonthly newsletter re-
porting and analyzing developments in Soviet
Estonia, was launched by Rein Taagepera. In
1973 it was renamed Baltic Events. Taagepera,
born in 1933 in Estonia, teaches political
science at the University of California,
Irvine.

Siberian-born Estonian sculptor Ferdinand L.
Weber won the competition to hew a statue of
Samuel de Champlain at the Vermont pavillion
at EXPO-67 in Montreal. Champlain was the
first European to set foot in Vermont and the
twelve-foot statue depicts him standing in a
canoe paddled by an Indian. The statue was
subsequently placed on Isle La Motte in Lake
Champlain. Weber, born in 1904, attended the
Estonian National School of Applied Arts in
Tallinn. He came to Vermont in 1952.

February 6. Andres Pranspill, a carpenter
and a journalist, died at the age of 80.
Pranspill left Estonia in 1909 as a sailor
and came to the United States the following
year. Trained as a navy paramedic, he completed high school in New York, studied a
variety of subjects at the City College of
New York and worked for a while for the newspaper Uus Ilm. In 1919 he passed the mate's
exam and went back to sea. During the 1920s
he worked as a carpenter and continued his
studies. In 1930 he went to work for an in-
surance company. Pranspill's main activity,
however, was Estonian-American societal life,
in which he always took a leading part. At
the same time, he was a correspondent for Estonian newspapers. Pranspill copyrighted the
term Välis-Eesti (Estonia Abroad) with the
Library of Congress in 1926 and began to issue
a periodical by that name. The first issue
was also the last. Pranspill's copyright
notwithstanding, the concept of Välis-Eesti
acquired a large following in the 1930s; it
provided an international context for Estonian ethnicity. In 1956 Pranspill published at
his own expense an Estonian Anthology which
he had compiled. He was his own best sales-
man and even sent several copies to European
heads of state, "from an American workingman,"
enclosing a bill for four dollars. Not all
obliged. Prince Rainier of Monaco sent his
copy back. His personal papers and archives
were donated to Estonian-American organizations, and they are a valuable source of information on Estonian history in the country,
especially during the first third of the
twentieth century.

Fall. Ivar Ivask assumed the editorship of
Books Abroad, a literary review issued by
the University of Oklahoma since 1927. He
was simultaneously appointed professor of
modern languages. Ivask, an Estonian born in
Latvia, began his studies at Marburg University in Germany and came to the United States
in 1949 to continue at the University of Minnesota, where he obtained his Ph.D. in 1954.
Ivask is also a poet in his own right, with
collections published in Estonian and German.

November. Estonian artist Rudolph Lepvalts
created all the huge animal floats for the
annual Macy's Thanksgiving Day Parade in New

York. He proceeded to do likewise in following years.

1968   The New York Estonian Lutheran Congregation of St. Matthew (Lexington Avenue) had grown from 100 members to 3,200 in twenty years under the leadership of the Reverend Rudolf Kiviranna. The congregation has existed continuously since 1898, when it was established by the Reverend Hans Rebane.

A survey of youth confirmed at Estonian congregations in America between 1952 and 1965 indicated that of those married, about two-thirds had non-Estonian spouses. Since most of the survey subjects were foreign born (although arriving in this country at an early age), the rate of intermarriage was unusually high. The survey also found that the group had a very high educational level, with individuals who had not completed high school or gone on to college a rarity. (See Table 3 in the Appendix.)

Endel J. Kolde's 680-page International Business Enterprise was published by Prentice-Hall. Kolde, born in Estonia in 1917, arrived in the United States in 1948, obtaining his Ph.D. from the University of Washington. He is on the faculty of that University and affiliated with its Bureau of Business Research.

Estonian-born mathematician Richard Härm, and his colleagues, astrophysicists Martin Schwarzchild and Robert H. Sanders, all of Princeton University, believed that they had discovered how heavier elements, such as silver and lead, were created. Härm, born in 1909, studied at the University of Tartu, and thereafter at the Max Planck Institute in Germany, receiving his Ph.D. from the University of Göttingen. He arrived in the United States after World War Two.

Rein Kilkson, on the faculty of Yale University, advanced a "Derivation Theory" in an attempt to prove Darwin's theory of evolution on a mathematical basis. The biophysicist was born in Estonia in 1927 and received his Ph.D. from Yale University in 1956. He has published extensively in the fields of molecular biophysics and viral structure. In

1972 Kilkson was appointed professor of physics at the University of Arizona.

February. The Legion of Estonian Liberation (Eesti Vabadusvõitlejate Liit) reissued a short English-language volume entitled Estonian War of Independence 1918-1920, which had been originally published in Estonia three decades earlier. The members of the legion are veterans, mostly of the World War Two era. The legion, organized in New York City in 1953, has 15 chapters across the country. (See Document No. 14.)

June 17. Peter Alexander [Peeter Aleksander] Speek died one day after his 95th birthday. Perhaps more than any other pre-World War One Estonian immigrant Speek was active in Estonian-American affairs. A socialist newspaper editor in Tsarist-ruled Estonia, Speek was forced into exile after the 1905 Revolution. Arriving in New York in 1908, he promptly participated in the founding of the Estonian-language socialist newspaper Uus Ilm. After his editorship of the newspaper from 1909 to 1910, Speek entered the University of Wisconsin at Madison, obtaining a master's degree in 1912 and a doctorate in 1915. His dissertation there, The Singletax and the Labor Movement, was published by the University of Wisconsin Press. Subsequently, Speek authored A Stake in the Land (Doubleday, Page and Company, 1922), a study on the investigation of immigrant settlers in the United States. He also wrote several sociological articles. Speek was furthermore a creative writer, who described his own piece, "Attaboy", as a "fanciful short story of two young Estonian boys and their sojourn in America as immigrants." Speek's pen however, was most proliferous in the Estonian press, both in Estonia and America, sprinkling it with liberal thinking. He took particular pride in his translation of the Estonian national anthem into English. Furthermore, Speek was one of the primary advocates of the Välis-Eesti (Estonia Abroad) concept, which he helped develop into an international movement between the two world wars. The concept provided the Estonians, no matter where they resided in the world, a unified basis of group identity in relation to the homeland in Estonia. For many years Speek

was employed at the Library of Congress in
Washington, D.C., as head of its Eastern European Division. His wife, Frances Valiant,
was a native of America. At their home in
Virginia, Speek had planted a native Estonian
birch.

November. Estonians participated in the American presidential elections for the first time
on an organized basis. Ilmar Heinaru of Michigan was chairman of the Nationalities Di-
vison of the Nixon for President Committee
and Arne Kalm of California was chairman of
Estonian-Americans for Nixon. In 1969 the
Heritage Groups Division of the Republican
National Committee requested that Kalm continue his efforts to organize Estonian-Americans for the Republican cause. In 1970 the
Estonian-American National Republican Committee was formed with Ilmar Pleer of New Jersey
as chairman. He was succeeded in 1972 by
Mati Kõiva of Connecticut and in 1974 by
Paul Saar of New York. By 1972 Estonian-American Republican Clubs existed in thirteen
states.

December 1. Scholars of Baltic ancestry laid
the groundwork for an organization speciali-
zing in Baltic studies, the Association for
the Advancement of Baltic Studies, at a conference at the University of Maryland. An
outgrowth of ideas advanced foremost by Janis
Gaigulis and the Association of Latvian Academic Fraternities, the initial academic conference was planned by a Steering Committee,
on which the Estonian representatives were
Herbert Valdsaar, Are Tsirk and Andres Jüriado. The association was incorporated in
1971 and has been very active in promoting
Baltic studies in the broadest meaning of the
term.

     Multidisciplinary conferences were held
afterward under the association's organization and cosponsorship at California State
College at San Jose (1970), the University
of Toronto (1972), and the University of Illinois at Chicago Circle (1974). The association has also sponsored several specialized
conferences, for example, two on language and
literature at Ohio State University (1970,
1972), and one on modern Baltic area history
at Stanford University and California State
University at San Jose (1973). Additionally,

the association has begun to publish the mul-
tidisciplinary Journal of Baltic Studies. At
the end of 1974 the association had about 700
members, some 200 of them being Estonian.
Scholars not of Baltic ancestry have also contributed to the association's conferences and
life.

1969   A meeting of organizational representatives,
scholars and other interested parties was
convened by the Estonian American National
Council to discuss the founding of an Estonian Archives in the United States. The idea
was unanimously adopted by the meeting, and
an advisory council was established with Heino
Taremäe as president. Actually, a collection
had already existed under the care of Ferdinand Kool in Connecticut for several years.
In 1974 the materials were moved into a spe-
cially erected building in Lakewood, New Jersey, where Ernst Luebik became the archivist.

Mihkel Suuberg, born in Estonia in 1911, was
named captain of the huge 326,000-ton tanker
Universe Portugal. Interestingly, the ves-
sel's sister ship, the Universe Kuwait, is under the command of another Estonian-born captain, Hans Ruben. Both make their homes in
the New York area.

June. A sociological study of Estonian youth
born in the United States and educated in
Lakewood, New Jersey, indicated that although
the youth had been raised in a bilingual and
bicultural social environment, they had no
special learning or personality problems. The
study examined religious participation, mental health, delinquency patterns, school performance and general personality adjustment.
     The study further indicated that Estonian
youth had a very high educational level. Of
those who had attended or graduated from Lakewood High School before 1965, only 10 percent
had ended their education at the high school
level. While 27 percent had some college education, fully 61 percent of the group had
completed college. Of those in the group,
19 percent had or were working toward various
master's degrees and 8 percent toward doctoral degrees. The study also uncovered the
fact that few of the young Estonian-Americans
remained in the Lakewood area after graduation
from high school or returned there after col-

lege. According to the study, the high rate
of geographical and educational mobility contributed to a high rate of intermarriage. Of
the Estonian youth confirmed at the Lakewood
Estonian Lutheran congregation between 1955
and 1965, and who were married by 1969, about
76 percent had non-Estonian spouses.

December. The New York Estonian Educational
Society celebrated its fortieth anniversary.
Founded in 1929 and incorporated in 1938,
the society's membership had grown from a
few hundred to nearly 1,000 in 1974. The society is the parent organization for numerous
other organizations such as the New York Estonian Theatre, the Estonian Supplementary
School, the New York Estonian Male Chorus,
the New York Estonian Female Chorus, and the
Estonian Philatelic Society. Additionally,
various athletic, modern dance, folk dance,
and other groups operate under its auspices,
as do also boy scout and girl scout units.
The society runs the Estonian House, which
provides a roof for almost all Estonian organizations in the New York metropolitan
area. In the early 1950s the society also
developed a property on Long Island as a
children's summer camp. The grounds of the
camp serve as a center for Estonian-American
activities "east of the city." Presently,
the society's president is Linold Milles.

December 13. The Estonian Music Center sponsored a special concert assembly in New York
City to commemorate the fiftieth anniversary
of the founding of the Tallinn Conservatory
in Estonia. The concert featured soprano
Helmi Betlem, pianists Dagmar Kokker and
Richard Anschütz, violinists Evi Liivak and
Valdeko Kangro, and cellist Kaljo Raid. Works
by both Estonian and non-Estonian composers
were presented. The featured speaker was a
graduate of the Tallinn Conservatory, Juta
Kurman, who is presently president of the
Estonian Music Center.
    At least five Estonians have received
doctoral degrees in music in the United
States during the 1950s and 1960s, and four
of them are on the faculties of universities:
Malle Mägi-Schultz, Arvi Sinka, Avo Sõmer,
Johannes Tall and Taavo Virkhaus. Additionally, a number of Estonian-Americans have
received professional master's degrees in

music.

THE 1970s: THE QUEST FOR NEW FORMS

1970   The United States census indicated that there
              were 20,507 first and second generation Esto-
              nians in the country.   In 1950 the figure had
              been 10,085 and in 1960 19,938.   The major
              change to be noted between the 1960 and 1970
              censuses was the decreasing importance of the
              first, or foreign born, generation.   In 1960
              70 percent of the group was foreign born; in
              1970 this was 59 percent.
                   No major changes have occurred in Estoni-
              an-American settlement patterns during the
              last ten years.   About one-half of the group
              still lived in the densely populated corridor
              between Boston and Washington, D.C.   However,
              there was a small decline in the number of
              Estonian-Americans in the Great Lakes area
              (including Minnesota):   from 3,696 in 1960
              to 3,446 in 1970.   At the same time the num-
              ber in the three West Coast states increased
              from 3,372 to 3,956.   There were large de-
              clines in three major Estonian-American cen-
              ters: Connecticut, from 1,000 to 825; New
              York, from 6,002 to 5,109; and Ohio, from
              674 to 528.   However, during the same decade
              there were increases in other centers: Cal-
              ifornia, from 2,572 to 2,871; Florida, from
              554 to 656; Oregon, from 310 to 562; Mary-
              land, from 515 to 884; and Massachusetts,
              from 402 to 688.
                   American censuses since 1930 have indi-
              cated that Estonians in the United States
              have lived primarily in the major industrial
              states.   And within these states they have
              always been residents of the larger urban
              areas or their suburban fringes.   (See Table
              4 in the Appendix.)

              Younger generation Estonian-American activ-
              ists in New York City decided to organize an
              annual cultural symposium named Kultuuri-
              päevad (Cultural Days).   To date, the four-
              day event over Easter weekend has been held
              five times.   The emphasis has been heavily
              cultural, and the programs have included
              concerts, theatre, films, and art displays,
              as well as scholarly lectures, panel discus-
              sions and seminars.   Some of the program has
              on occasion been in English in order to at-

tract both non-Estonians and the intermarried and their spouses. The event has been designed specifically to appeal more to the younger generation than the older, and participants have come from all over the United States and Canada. Those active in the organization of the symposium have included: Mardi Valgemäe, Heino Ainso, Liivi Jōe, Juhan Kurrik, and Andres Kurrik.

Valvo Raag, an Estonian-born electrical engineer, developed a new and unique battery with a life of ten to twenty years. The battery became especially useful for heart pacemakers, where battery life previously was a mere one to two years.

Endel Tulving was appointed a full professor of psychology at Yale University. Born in Estonia in 1927, he graduated from the University of Toronto and received a Ph.D. from Harvard University in 1957. An experimental psychologist, Tulving is an expert on storage and retrieval processes in human memory. His many publications include the coeditorship of Organization of Memory (1972). During 1972 and 1973 Tulving was a resident fellow at the Center for Advanced Study in the Behavioral Sciences, Stanford, California.

March 7. The Parent-Teachers Association of the Estonian Supplementary School in New York City confirmed a plan advocated by Victor Obet and Alfred Jōks to found a fund which would provide centralized financial assistance to the network of Estonian-American Supplementary Schools. On November 8, 1970, the Estonian School Fund in the United States was incorporated in the State of New York, with the primary aim of promoting the study of Estonian language and culture. Although to date the fund has been only accumulating capital, it has already begun to provide financial support to activities as diverse as the teaching of Estonian to the spouses and children of intermarried Estonians (as well as to Estonian teenagers) and the publication of a teaching methods handbook for Estonian Supplementary School teachers, prepared by an Estonian educational specialist in Sweden.

April. The oldest Estonian organization continually in existence, Eesti Üliōpilaste

Selts (Estonian Students Association), celebrated its one-hundreth anniversary. It was
founded in Estonia by student activists at
the University of Tartu to facilitate their
study of the Estonian people's history and
culture, topics absent from the German and
Russian-controlled university's curriculum.
When the Soviet Union annexed Estonia in the
summer of 1940, the association was banned.
But it continued to exist and grow in exile
and in 1973 had 735 members, with 235 of
them living in the United States. Most of
the present members of the association joined after 1944. The main commemorative cere-
monies of the association's centennial were
held in New York City, bringing together
members from around the world for several
days of assemblies, concerts and social
events. In 1974 the association furthermore
celebrated the ninetieth anniversary of its
blue-black-white tricolor, which had become
the official colors of the flag of the Republic of Estonia.

October. The Estonian academic fraternity
Rotalia sponsored a special public discussion on issues of assimilation in the Estonian-American community. One of the conclu-
sions of the three-hour discussion was that
intermarriage and cultural assimilation are
inevitable given the Estonians' small population size, their geographical dispersion,
high educational level, and rapid social mobility. It was recommended that the community attempt to realize this and to adapt to
the realities. It was furthermore suggested
that the community not isolate the large
group of intermarried youth, but that it attempt, rather, to draw them closer to the
social and cultural life of the community by
sponsoring occasional English-language events.
     Estonian academic fraternities have
been active in the United States since 1949,
carrying on traditions established in Estonia prior to World War Two. Chapters of
twelve fraternities, with a total membership of about 800, united in 1950 to form the
League of Estonian Fraternities in the United
States (Eesti Korporatsioonide Liit). The
league also is a continuation of traditions
existing in prewar Estonia. Among its many
activities the league has provided financial
support to a variety of Estonian organiza-

tions dealing with scholarly, cultural, political and youth affairs. The League also
donated money, materials, and labor during
the 1960s to partially rebuild the New York
Estonian House, where it has been headquartered. The fraternity Rotalia is the largest
in the League in terms of membership. A
number of Estonian academic sororities have
also continued their activities in the United
States.

1971   One part of the lunar vehicle remaining on
the moon bore the inscription: "Harald Oliver -- Estonian." Oliver, born in the United
States of Estonian parents, was an engineer
who helped construct the moon vehicle. Estonians have also been active in other phases
of the space program. For example, Jyri
Kork, born in Estonia in 1927, coauthored the
pioneering Design Guide to Orbital Flight
(1962). He is presently head of the Dynamics
and Advanced Missions Analysis Branch of the
"Delta Project" at the Goddard Space Flight
Center in Greenbelt, Maryland. Rein Ise,
born in Estonia in 1935, headed the Apollo
Telescope Mount Project at the Marshall Space
Flight Center in Alabama, for which he received a special service medal. In 1974 Ise
was named director of the "Skylab" project.
Both Kork and Ise received their higher education in America after World War Two.
        The goodwill messages taken to the moon
by American astronauts in 1969 included one
which read: "The people of Estonia join those
who hope and work for freedom and a better
world." It was signed by Ernst Jaakson, consul general of the Republic of Estonia in the
United States. And on March 21, 1972, the
Estonian American National Council received a
letter from Senator Charles H. Percy of Illinois which stated: "The Department of State
has assured me that the flags of free Lithuania, Latvia and Estonia, among others, will
be implanted on the moon during the flight of
Apollo XVI in May of this year..."

Jüri Kaude was appointed a professor of radi-
ology at the University of Florida at Gainesville. Born in Estonia in 1921, Kaude received his medical education at the University of Kiel in Germany and the University of
Lund in Sweden. Internationally known in his
field, Kaude has published over 100 scientif-

ic articles in American, British, German, and
Swedish medical journals.

Alan Tomson, born in the United States of Estonian parents and probably the first Estonian-American to have attended the United
States Military Academy at West Point, set
two new academy records. He broke the 200-
yard swim mark by twenty-four seconds and
the record for combined competition (marks-
manship, running and swimming) by two seconds.

April. The first Estonian play in English
translation performed in the United States
on the legitimate stage premiered at the
off-Broadway La Mama E.T.C. Entitled The
Cinderella Game (originally Tuhkatriinu
Mäng), the play was authored by the young Soviet Estonian playwright Paul-Eerik Rummo.
It was translated into English by Andres Männik and Mardi Valgemäe. As Professor Valgemäe has noted: "Instead of a storybook Cinderella and her Prince Charming, there are
several pretenders to these titles...[The]
characters in Rummo's play ask, 'Who am I?'
The answer seems to be that they are simply
puppets playing interchangeable roles in a
meaningless game." The play is an example
of the theatre of the absurd.

May. The Voice of America's Estonian Service entered its twentieth year of broadcast
activities in the Estonian language. The service was initially headed by Kaarel R. Pusta,
Jr. (1951-1957), and thereafter by Jaan Kitzberg (1957-1974) and Voldemar Veedam (1975
to the present). The service beams two half-
hour length broadcasts to Soviet Estonia daily.
These include news, commentary on the news,
and frequent reports on Estonian activities in
the Western world. The United States Congress
recently appropriated funds for additional
Estonian-language broadcasts, which will begin
in July, 1975, through Radio Liberty.
what goes on in the world.

July. The American Chamber Music Festival at
Thiel College, in Greenville, Pennsylvania,
was organized by an Estonian-born member of
the music faculty, Ivan Romanenko. He came
to the United States in 1949 and was concert-
master of the National Symphony Orchestra in

Washington, D.C. for sixteen years. Romanenko's wife, Carmen Prii, also from Estonia, is
an accomplished concert violinist. Premier-
ing at the festival was Vladimir Padwa's [Pad-
va] String Quartet. Although born in Russia
in 1900, Padwa moved to Estonia at an early
age and received his education there. He was
one of the founders of the Estonian National
Conservatory in Tallinn. He came to the United States in the early 1930s and soon began
to accompany violinist Mischa Elman on his
concert tours. An accomplished pianist, Padwa was a founder and member of the First Piano Quartet and has recorded for RCA Victor
records. He has been the winner of the Madri-
gal Society and Peabody awards, and he has
composed symphonies, piano concertos, chamber
music and a ballet entitled Tom Sawyer. Presently, Padwa teaches music at New York University.

September. The New York weekly Vaba Eesti
Sõna reported that a social gathering of intermarried Estonians and their families took
place at the Chicago Estonian House. It attracted over 200 people, as did a similar
event the following year. The first such social event in 1970 had been a picnic attended
by 150 people. There was talk of forming an
Association of Intermarried Estonians. In
the spring of 1973 the same source reported a
similar gathering in the Washington, D.C.,
area.

1972   William S. Hein and Company of Buffalo reprinted the 537-page Congressional report entitled Baltic States: A Study of Their Origin and National Development; Their Seizure
and Incorporation into the U.S.S.R. The
work was originally published in 1954 as the
third interim report of the Select Committee
on Communist Aggression in the House of Representatives, popularly known as the Kersten
Committee. The committee had been originally
formed specifically to investigate the Soviet
takeover of the Baltic states. The Estonian-
American community had called for the formation of such a committee as early as 1945
(see Document No. 9). The United States Congress has always taken a sympathetic stand on
Baltic issues, and resolutions have been introduced and adopted on several occasions
(see Document No. 16).

As Väino Riismandel noted in the periodical Võitlev Eesti (Fighting Estonia) in
1956, in an article dealing with the Kersten
Committee, the Estonian-American community
cooperated extensively with the committee,
providing witnesses and documents. Võitlev
Eesti, published in New York by the Committee
for a Free Estonia between 1952 and 1956 and
edited by Adolf Perandi, Ilmar Raamot, and
Evald Roosaare, itself provided important
informational services on issues pertinent to
the Congressional investigation and to cur-
rent news items relevant to Soviet Estonia.

The Estonian Centre of the International
P.E.N. Club, the world-wide organization of
creative writers, essayists and publicists,
transferred its operations from Sweden to the
United States. Founded in Estonia in 1928,
the centre has existed outside the country
since 1944. In 1974 the centre had 42 active
members, of whom 14 resided in the United
States. Since 1940 a significant amount of
Estonian-language literature has been produced in the Western countries.
     One of the active leaders of the centre
in the United States has been Asta Willmann-
Linnolt of Farmington, Connecticut. She is
known in Estonian literary circles for her
novels, but she has been also active in the
local theatre as a producer at the New Britain Repertory Theatre. One of her own plays
premiered there in late 1972.

Mardi Valgemäe's Accelerated Grimace: Expressionism in the American Drama of the 1920s
was published. It was hailed by one reviewer
as the most significant work on the subject
of expressionism in American theatre. Valgemäe, born in Estonia in 1935, received his
Ph.D. from the University of California at
Los Angeles in 1964, and since 1968 he has
been a professor of English at Lehman College of the City University of New York. He
was promoted to full professor in 1974.

August E. Komendant's 640-page Contemporary
Concrete Structures was published by McGraw-
Hill. Komendant, born in Estonia, came to
the United States after World War Two. He
was a consulting engineer for Habitat-67 at
the Montreal Expo-67. Komendant has collabo-
rated with such prominent architects as Kahn

and Saarinen.

June. The Hillsborough County Court in New
Hampshire convicted twenty-one-year-old student radical Jaan Karl Laaman for fire-bomb-
ing the Manchester police and fire building
on February 16, 1972. He was sentenced to
fourteen to twenty years at hard labor. Laaman is of Estonian descent.

June 16. The University of Maryland conducted
a special assembly, where Dr. Ernst Öpik presented a lecture on the moon's morphology and
evolution. The purpose of the assembly was
to award Öpik a special gold medal "for distinguished achievements and important contributions to the understanding of the origin
of the solar system and the planets." Only
six such gold medals were struck jointly by
the American Association for the Advancement
of Science and the Meteoritic Society to commemorate the 400th anniversary of the birth
of Johannes Kepler. Öpik had been unable to
attend the regular award ceremony the preceding winter. Born in Estonia, Öpik received
a doctoral degree from the University of
Tartu there in astronomy in 1923. After
World War Two he settled in Ireland, where he
has worked at the Armagh Observatory. However, for over two decades he has spent approximately one-half of each year as a visiting professor in the Department of Physics
and Astronomy at the University of Maryland.
A distinguished scientist of international
stature, Öpik has 274 major scientific works
to his credit, complemented by 520 minor
ones (as of 1972). One of his best-known
works was The Oscillating Universe (1960,
Mentor Books). It is to be noted, additionally, that Öpik is an accomplished amateur musician, having even written several symphonies.

Summer. A world-wide social and cultural
festival Eesti Päevad (Estonian Days) was
held in Toronto, Canada, and attended by Estonians from all over the Western world,
with charter flights or groups coming from
Sweden, West Germany, Great Britain and Australia. It is estimated that 25,000 Estonians participated in the festivities, including thousands from the United States, both as

observers and performers. The week-long festivities included all types of cultural and
social events. Several political rallies
were held under the slogan "Freedom for Estonia." The latter were addressed by former
Canadian Prime Minister John Diefenbaker,
and the then Foreign Minister Mitchell Sharp.
Many families, as well as friends, were re-
united for the first time since fleeing their
homeland during World War Two.

November. Estonian-Americans took an active
part in the national elections and, in some
cases, in local elections. A network of
Estonian-American Republican Clubs had sprung
up in thirteen states around the country
since the 1968 elections. Estonians headed
the state-wide Republican effort among ethnic
groups in four key electoral states: California (Arne Kalm), Indiana (Ilo Johanson), New
Jersey (Ilmar Pleer), and Connecticut (Mati
Kõiva). Anne Treumuth, one of the very few
Estonian-Americans to actually run for office,
was elected as a Republican to the Jackson
Township Municipal Council in New Jersey.
There has been a virtual absence of organized
support among Estonian-Americans for the Democratic Party.

November 18. The presidents of the following
three organizations -- the Estonian World
Council, the Supreme Committee for the Liberation of Lithuania, and the World Federation
of Free Latvians -- issued a declaration of
principles in New York City, which subsequently led to the formation of a Baltic World
Conference. Its primary purpose was stated
as follows: "By joint and mutually agreed action to help the Estonian, Latvian and Lithuanian nations free themselves from Soviet-
Russian occupation that is threatening the
very physical and cultural existence of the
Baltic people." Alfred Anderson signed the
declaration on behalf of the Estonians. In
1974 the leadership of the new organization
was in the hands of Estonians, with Ilmar
Pleer as its president. Pleer was simultaneously president of the Estonian American
National Council.

1973   Alvine Kingo turned 100. She appears to be
the first Estonian to have lived to such a
great age in the United States. Kingo re-

sided with her seventy-six-year-old daughter in Fort Collins, Colorado, where her next-door grandson was a professor at Colorado State University. She arrived in the United States in 1949.

September. Nineteen-year-old Toomas Edur of Estonian descent became a member of the Cleveland Crusaders hockey team.

September. Hardu Keck's first showing in New York City took place at the Warren Gallery in Greenwich Village. Keck was also one of four artists to receive a prize of five-hundred dollars at the Sixth Art Festival in Rhode Island, held at Providence in 1964, an event with over 900 works exhibited by 300 artists. Keck, born in Estonia in 1940, holds a Master of Fine Arts degree from the Rhode Island School of Design, where he is currently on the faculty. His works have been displayed both in the United States and in Europe. Keck's acrylic corner paintings appear to defy both perspective and gravity, and he has also experimented with abstract neon sculptures.

Fall. The international quarterly of literature, Books Abroad, published by the University of Oklahoma, devoted an issue to Baltic literature. It contained four essays on Estonian topics. Another literary quarterly, Literary Review, published by Fairleigh Dickinson University in New Jersey, had published a special Baltic issue already in the spring of 1965.

1974   Ilse Lehiste became the elected president of the Association for the Advancement of Baltic Studies, a United States based international scholarly organization. A professor of linguistics at Ohio State University, Lehiste is the first woman to head the 700 member association. A graduate of the University of Tartu in Estonia, Lehiste received a doctoral degree from the University of Hamburg in Germany in 1948 and a second doctoral degree from the University of Michigan in 1959. Her many publications include the monograph Consonant Quantity and Phonological Units in Estonian (1966).
    Estonian women in America have an appreciably higher educational level than the

country's female population in general. In
1968 a survey indicated that only 14 percent
of Estonian-American women aged 23 to 33 had
stopped their education at the high school
level. While 25 percent had some college education but no degree, a high 61 percent were
college graduates. Of the whole group, 15
percent had or were working on a master's degree and 5 percent on a doctoral degree. Estonian-American women are to be found in most
professions, and quite a few are on university faculties. The first Estonian woman in
the United States to have received a doctoral
degree appears to have been Elizabeth Judas
in 1941 from Columbia University. Her publications include the books Russian Influ-
ences on Estonian Literature (1941) and Ras-
putin (1942).

Estonian women have also held important
leadership posts in ethnic organizations. For
example, Vaike Lugus has been a president of
the Connecticut Estonian Society and a vice
president of the Estonian American National
Council. Virve Puström, a second generation
Estonian in the country, for several terms
has been president of the Lakewood Estonian
Association. Urve Auksi has been a long-time
head of the Midwest Estonian Youth Association and Kadri Niider of New York is the president of the Estonian Students Fund in the
United States.

Victor Terras' Belinsky and Russian Literary
Criticism was published. Terras, born in Es-
tonia in 1921, has also authored The Young
Dostoevsky (1969). He arrived in the United
States after World War Two and received a
Ph.D. from the University of Chicago in 1963.
Presently he is a professor and the chairman
of the Department of Slavic Languages and Li-
terature at Brown University.

January. A report issued by the coordinating
organization, Eesti Koolide Keskus (Estonian
Schools Center), indicated that there were
fifteen Estonian Supplementary Schools in the
United States, in localities from Seattle to
Baltimore and Los Angeles to Hartford, with a
total of 392 pupils and 98 teachers. Although
one such school already existed as part of the
New York Estonian Educational Society before
World War Two, the present ones were all founded afterwards, mostly in the early 1950s. Their

major objective has always been to teach the
Estonian language. The center itself has coordinated instructional materials, which are
prepared in part in Sweden and Canada, and it
has conducted several pedagogical refresher
seminars. The center has functioned under
the leadership of Gaston Randvee of Willimant-
tic, Connecticut.

March 17. Louis Kahn, the "humble titan of
world architecture," died. Kahn was born on
February 20, 1901, on the Estonian island of
Saaremaa [then Ösel] and arrived in the United States in 1905. In 1924 he obtained a
degree in architecture from the University of
Pennsylvania and in 1964 was granted a Doctor
of Architecture degree from the Polytechnical
Institute of Milan, Italy. Kahn also was on
the faculty of Yale University in 1947-1948
and later at the University of Pennsylvania.
Kahn designed buildings in relation to the
inner order by which he believed people inter-
act. He had a reverence for natural light and
brought the workday metabolics of buildings --
the mechanical equipment, stair towers, and
other elements which architecture had hidden
for centuries -- into the open. Among his
most famous architectural landmarks are the
Library of Phillips Exeter Academy, the Kim-
bell Art Museum in Fort Worth, Texas, the Yale
Art Gallery, the Institute of Management at
Ahmedabad, and the Capital of Bangladesh at
Dacca. After his death, it was announced that
one of his last designs was a memorial to
Franklin Delano Roosevelt on Roosevelt Island
in New York City. The bulk of the memorial
will be a park, which converges toward a
"room" of granite at the tip of the island,
with the fourth side open to the East River
and a view. The granite "room" will have an
abstract sculpture, and outside, facing the
park, will be a bust of the former president.
Quotations will be carved on the granite be-
side the sculptures, while the rest of the
walls will be blank.

June. Estonian academic fraternities, sororities and student associations held their
third joint Summer Days in Lakewood, New Jersey. Cooperation among the various student
organizations, sometimes lacking in the old
country, has become increasingly more common.
The New York Estonian weekly Vaba Eesti Sõna

noted that there was an unusually high attendance on the part of the "younger generation."

June. Anton Männik, who left Estonia in
1944, dedicated a brand new building-block
factory at his enterprise, Lakewood Super
Block Company, in New Jersey. With a capacity for 27,000 building blocks per day, the
plant is the largest of its type on the East
Coast. It is one of the few large businesses
which Estonian-Americans of the postwar period have founded, although there are many Estonian building and masonry contractors in
the Lakewood Area.

July. The twentieth annual Estonian Athletic
Games on the East Coast were held at Lakewood,
New Jersey, under the traditional sponsorship
of the local Estonian community and the Estonian Athletic League in the United States
(Eesti Spordiliit Ühendriikides). The games
have provided for competition in almost every
athletic endeavor, both in individual and
team sports, and have usually drawn up to
several thousand participants and spectators.
Similar events have been also held on the
West Coast, and Estonian, Latvian and Lithuanian athletic organizations in the United
States and Canada have periodically held
"Baltic Olympics." Those active in the leadership of the Estonian Athletic League have
included: Aleksander Prima, Raimond Pals,
Bernhard Parming, Heino Maasikas, and Ferdinand Tammann.

July. Twelve-year old Seattlean Eve Kosen-
kranius, of Estonian descent, broke the American 1,500 meter swim record for her age
group with a time of 17:32.2 at Santa Clara,
California.

July. Under Estonian leadership, exile boy
and girl scout units of Estonian, Latvian,
Lithuanian, Polish, Ukrainian and Hungarian
ancestry held a joint camp, Unity-74, at the
Estonian Scouting Reservation in Jackson,
New Jersey. The camp was headed by Estonian
scoutmaster Harry Tarmo, and girl scout leader Anu-Irja Parming was program director.

August. Tõnu Kalam, a twenty-seven-year-old
Estonian-born musician currently on the faculty of the University of Nevada at Reno,

conducted the closing number at the Marlboro
Musical Festival in Massachusetts. In earlier years his work has been performed at the
festival, where his father, Endel Kalam of
Boston, has coordinated sessions in chamber
music. The elder Kalam, associated with Boston University, heads the New England Chamber
Quartet.

September. An Estonian-American developer,
Rudolf Susi, with the participation of local
dignitaries, dedicated Lake Endla in New York
State near the village of Modena. The lake,
on a 240-acre tract, was named for one in
central   Estonia, and apparently is the
third American lake to carry an Estonian name.

December. The Estonian-language weekly newspaper New Yorgi Postimees (The New York Courier), published and edited by August Kärsna,
completed its tenth year with a circulation
of 800. New York City presently also has two
other Estonian-language newspapers and one
periodical. The Uus Ilm was founded in 1909
(see page 11), the Vaba Eesti Sõna in 1949
(see page 32), and the magazine Meie Tee in
1931 (see page 19).

1975   January. The annual Väliseestlase kalender
(Calendar for the Estonian Abroad), published
for over two decades by Nordic Press in New
York City and edited by Erich Ernits, reported
that there were at least 106 Estonian medical
doctors and dentists in the United States.
This is approximately one doctor for every
200 first and second generation Estonian-Americans. About 25-percent of the doctors are
women. Most of the doctors have received
their professional education in the United
States during the last twenty-five years. The
1975 calendar also listed 5 veterinary doctors, 10 lawyers and 23 architects.

January 24. A newly elected Representative
Assembly of the Estonian American National
Council convened in New York City for its annual meeting. The fifty-delegate assembly has
been elected every three years by the Estonian-American community, and about 4,000 people
have voted in each of the elections since
1952. The assembly elected Ilmar Pleer of
New Jersey to a second term as president of
the council. The 1974 financial statement

of the council indicated that during the past few years the Estonian-American community has contributed about $30,000 annually to support its activities. As late as 1969 the council's annual budget had been $15,000 and in 1961 only $7,000. The organization's 1975 budget, furthermore, suggested an important shift in priorities. Namely, for the first time, the council has budgeted more money for programs dealing with Estonian culture and youth activities than for those dealing with political affairs. (See also entry on page 37.)

1976   The second Estonian World Festival will be held in July in Baltimore, with preparatory work done by the members of the Baltimore Estonian Society. Participants are expected from as far away as Australia and Sweden. The first such festival in 1972 was in Toronto and attracted 25,000 Estonians from around the world. Festivities will include all types of cultural events, social gatherings and political rallies, and will be related to the United States bicentennial celebration. (See Document No. 20.)

Document 1

THE ARRIVAL OF THE REVEREND HANS REBANE IN THE UNITED
STATES, 1896

> The following translation of the
> lead article of the first issue
> of the first Estonian-language
> newspaper in the United States,
> published in New York City, tells
> how Reverend Rebane arrived in
> the country and began to seek out
> individual Estonians.
>
> Source: Eesti Amerika Postimees
> (The Estonian-American Courier),
> March, 1897.

From earliest times America has been the place where
the sons and daughters of all of the world's people have
come to seek happiness. In recent times, Estonians, too,
have begun to immigrate to the United States to seek opportunity and a new life, to look at America's beauty.
It has been about a year since I arrived here. It
was on January 2, 1896, that I first had the pleasure of
seeing the country, namely, in New York City, with its
skyscrapers. All of the worry and the tribulations of the
stormy ocean voyage were now forgotten. Everywhere there
were happy faces and kindly gazes. The immigration officials and a doctor had met us at sea, and they quickly
finished their work. It was not long before our ship, the
Saale, docked, and every traveler who did not have a
problem went his or her way. A representative of the Lutheran Pilgrimage House [Lutherisches Pilger Haus] came
to meet me at the harbor, and I spent my first night in
America there, resting from the weary voyage.
On the second day I talked with the Reverend Keyl,
director of the Lutheran Pilgrimage House, about mission
work among Latvian and Estonian immigrants in New York,
as well as in other cities, for which purpose the [German
Lutheran] Missouri Synod President Brand had invited me
here. Reverend Keyl informed me that there were a goodly
number of Latvians in New York City, but to date he had
heard nothing about Estonians. He gave me the addresses
of some Latvians, and took me to meet the first of them
personally, since the city was strange to me. They in
turn introduced me to others. Thus, already on January
5 I could deliver my first sermon in Latvian at the Pilgrimage House. Here I also met two Estonian men, Jonson
and Gutman, who knew Latvian and who mixed with the Lat-

vians socially. I asked them immediately about other Estonians in the city, but they did not know of any.

From New York I soon went to Boston where a goodly
number of Latvians awaited me and received me joyously.
I delivered a sermon in their language and inquired if
there might also be Estonians in the city. They said
that there were some Estonians about fifty miles west of
Boston working in a factory, and I went there. However,
except for one man, there were no Estonians here [Wor-
cester?], but I found Finns and Poles. The only Estonian
there was away at the time, and no one could tell me when
he might return. Back in Boston, I advertised in the
German newspaper New England for Estonians, asking that
they contact me. Unfortunately, to date I have found not
one Estonian in Boston, although there are several Finns.
Counting children, there are about 300 Latvians here.

From Boston I traveled to Philadelphia, where again
many Latvians awaited me. And here, too, I inquired
about Estonians. It was a great pleasure for me to find
one Estonian family, the J.Bartel-s, and two bachelors,
A. Kaasik and M[...], and to give holy communion to a
sick Finnish woman. I also heard that there were Estonians in the city of Wilmington, about thirty miles to
the south, namely, two brothers, P. and M. Kivisaar.
But I have not yet had the opportunity to locate them.
Hopefully I can do so in the future.

From Philadelphia I went to Baltimore, where about
50 Latvians awaited me and received me joyfully. And
here it was again my pleasure to meet an Estonian among
them, K. Pilberg, to whom I gave communion. He was a
tailor by trade, but he could barely earn a living by
it. Because of this he had become a merchant seaman and
now sails the oceans.

From Baltimore I returned to New York, where I have
now become acquainted with the Finnish pastor, Reverend
Durchmann. Like myself, he also travels to other cities. With his permission I set up an address-book re-
gistry for Estonians at the Finnish Seamen's House at
53 Beaver Street. I asked that every Estonian visiting
the House leave his name and address. It has been thus
possible for me to obtain some addresses of Estonians,
most of these being seamen. Those who live in the city
work in the factories and some are servants for the
wealthy.

An Estonian, J. Gutman, has for some years been a
trolley operator in Brooklyn, for which he receives good
wages. Another, Mihkel Pai, is a carpenter. He lives
in Brooklyn and with God's help has advanced so far as
to work independently and he is able even to give work to
others. I have talked with him for several hours about
how we could locate Estonian brothers and sisters in this
foreign land. He said that he would gladly help me in

this task, and he has devotedly begun to look for other Estonians in New York and Brooklyn.

Through the German pastor, Reverend Keyl, I met an Estonian, August Bostrom, who comes from [the city of] Pärnu. God has blessed his progress in America, and he is employed by the Immigration Service as an inspector. His job is to question new immigrants. I talked with him about mission work among Estonians in North America, and he wished me luck in this, promising to assist. His wife, who is a very good piano and harmonica player, kindly promised to play for me during Estonian and Latvian services...

Document 2

ESTONIAN-AMERICAN LIFE DURING THE 1920s

The following translations from
Estonian periodicals published in
Tallinn, Estonia, give a glimpse
of Estonian-American life in the
United States during the 1920s.

Source: Eesti Hõim (The Estonian
Tribe), No. 4, 1928; and Välis
Eesti Almanak (The Almanac for
Estonians Abroad), Volume 1, 1929.

The majority of the Estonians in America are arti-
sans. First place belongs to carpenters, a craft in which
the Estonians appear to be particularly skillful, followed by ironworkers, tailors and painters. The women are
mostly housemaids, waitresses and seamstresses. The oldest among the male workers here are mostly union members.
Entrepreneurs and businessmen are in the minority,
most of them work as independent builders-contractors or
profit from real estate transactions...Whole streets have
been built by Estonians in [the New York suburbs of] Bo-
gota and Teaneck [in New Jersey]...It is said that in California there are more Estonians in business ventures
than in New York. Thus, in San Francisco there are about
forty Estonian businesses...
Speaking of the Estonians' line of work in America,
one should not omit those here who have purchased farms
and have taken up agriculture. Farther inland, for in-
stance in Wisconsin, Montana, Oregon, Washington and elsewhere, one can find Estonian settlements with a dozen or
more families...
Estonian professional people who come to the United
States to seek employment as doctors, lawyers or school-
teachers have only occasionally been able to find it...
The main obstacle is the language...

Compared to Europe, the pay is much higher here.
Thus, a carpenter earns $12 a day, a locksmith $8 to $10,
a bricklayer $14 to $16, and so forth. But circumstances
here do not permit much more for these wages than adequate living, which, however, is on the average better,
of course, than in Estonia. A suit here costs $40, a
pair of good boots or shoes $8 (one can also get $2.50
boots and they wear well), a shirt $1.50 and a hat $2 to
$5. Food costs a single person about $10 to $12 a month,
for a family $15 to $18.

The question of education and further study is re-
garded by the oldtimers here as a waste of time which is
better not to be bothered with. The young ones are not
given a penny's worth of moral support. The men who have
arrived more recently, after World War One, are quite
eager and try hard to advance, but most of them have low-
er wages than the old unionized workers...

It must be noted that the children of Estonians who
are born in America do not know, in the main, a single
word of Estonian...About a third of the Estonians...are
owners of cars.

Document   3

ESTONIAN-AMERICAN LIFE IN NEW YORK CITY, 1932

The following translation from
an Estonian-language monthly published in New York City gives a
glimpse of Estonian life there
in the early 1930s.

Source: Meie Tee (Our Path),
November, 1932.

An estimated 4,000 Estonians live in New York...The
largest single concentration is to be found in Harlem,
with only a few Estonians in the Mid-town area.
During the past two years a large number of New York
Estonians returned to their homeland...It is not known
how many remained in Estonia for good and how many came
back.
Working conditions in New York are nothing to crow
about. Construction is at a total standstill. Most Estonian carpenters and bricklayers have either switched
to other fields of endeavor or have journeyed to the
homeland, or have returned to sea, their former means of
a livelihood. Only a few have remained true to their
trade here. They work a few days a week and get $3-$5-
$7 for an eight-hour day. Painting jobs can still be
found, but no emphasis is placed on the wages received.
The novice painter is paid $3.20 to $4 for an eight-hour
day, the experienced ones earn $5 to $6. But during the
past ten years so many new buildings have gone up that
there is no fear of an apartment shortage for the next
ten. During the past two years the rent has dropped
about twenty per cent.
Many Estonian families, after the husband has lost
his job, have become residential building superinten-
dents. The "super" gets $20 to $65 in monthly wages
plus two rooms, a kitchen and bath in a four to five-
story house with 15 to 40 apartments. The actual work
then is done by the wife, while the husband looks for
work outside. But even these jobs have become more
scarce recently, and the wages have dropped.
Many young Estonians have also switched to working
in buildings. Since the days of good pay are gone, one
agrees to a small wage as long as the job is secure.
Thus, many are employed in New York apartment and office-
buildings and get the following wages: elevator operator,
$75 to $80 monthly for a twelve-hour workday; doorman,
same conditions; boilerroom furnace attendant, $75 to $80
plus a free apartment; porter, $65 to $70 monthly for a

ten-hour workday.   All depends on the size of the building and the part of town in which it is located.

New York Estonian lasses work mostly in homes, except for those whose English is fluent, who mostly are
in other occupations.   Housemaids, as beginners, get $25
to $40 monthly plus room and board in a good home.   Those
with some experience get $50 to $60 and the best jobs pay
up to $85 a month plus room and board.   But then one has
to be fully experienced: know how to cook, to take full
care of the house by oneself, and to answer phone calls...

Estonian women here have always worked, even though
the husband might have a well-paying job.   Perhaps this
is because of an established tradition.

One hears very little about Estonians getting married in New York.   There is no way of knowing whose fault
this is.   It is said that the Estonian lasses here have a
hard time finding a husband.   But wherever you look you
can find an old bachelor roaming about, downcast.   Those
who "make out" with the tender sex don't care about mar-
riage, since most lack a good income and therefore find
it difficult to get a wife...Since men have little work,
one lives from day to day, like a bird in a tree, occasionally half-hungry.

As few as the Estonians in America are, they are
split into two camps.   Both factions are headquartered in
New York.   Moreover, they are in the same neighborhood,
only a couple of streets apart.   So close, that a good
man could cast a stone from one camp to the other.   But
in one there waves a red banner, and in the other the
blue-black-white flag [of Estonia].   The American government does not prevent the activity of either, it just
looks on and smiles...

Document   4

ESTONIANS IN AMERICA,   1939

The following commentary was written by Herbert Haljaspõld in an
English-language newspaper published in Tallinn, Estonia.

Source: Baltic Times, September,
1939

There are reputed to be some sixty thousand Estonians in North America, most of whom live in the U.S.A....
There are unfortunately no reliable statistics available.
All we have in this respect is a collection of data of
some 2500 Estonian families in North America, compiled ten
years ago, by Mr. K. Kuusik, then of the Estonian Consulate General in New York. For this reason the estimate of
60,000 must be taken with reserve, as it is not impossible
that a detailed scrutiny might cut it by 50%...
    Estonian emigration to North America is not old. More
recent still is the beginning of any information in the
Estonian press concerning Estonian settlements there.
Probably the first Estonians settled in North America during the final quarter of the last century...Information
sent by Finnish clergy in America to Dr. Oscar Kallas, who
was later Estonian envoy in London, appeared in Postimees
[The Courier; a Tartu, Estonia, newspaper] No. 284 of 20th
Nov. 1896. A significant portion of this news referred to
seven Estonian farmer families in Dakota, who had arrived
there some years earlier from the Crimea. Not infrequent-
ly Estonian farmers went to America after first emigrating
into the interior of Russia.
    Later to these emigrant farmers who looked for bet-
ter farming opportunities in America, were added industrial workers and artificers. The main flow of emigrants
commenced only after the abortive Russian Revolution of
1905, which was suppressed. In most American towns, but
principally in the Eastern states and on the Pacific
coast, Estonians singly and in groups of a few score appeared in the industrial districts. There were larger
numbers of Estonians in New York, New Jersey, and Philadelphia, as well as in all parts of Pennsylvania, and in
Boston and the New England States. Many settled farther
west around Chicago, and smaller numbers in the states
of Ohio and California, and in the cities of St. Louis
and New Orleans. Only a few scattered Estonians were
attracted to the Rocky Mountains.
    It was a chaotic and unorganized movement which
took Estonians to America. The chief reason was the

narrow economic conditions prevailing at home under the
Czarist regime and the fable of easy life across the ocean.
Other factors were letters from friends and relations who
had settled earlier in America and the propaganda of the
shipping lines.

In these tiny new Estonian settlements there was
no inner tie, no common feeling. No relations were maintained between the various social groups. The majority
of the settlers were industrial workers, often unskilled,
and agricultural labourers, who had to start earning
their living by heavy labour. There were few skilled
workers, few professional men or merchants. The few who
were better educated and got better jobs were not out-
standing among their compatriots. Social equilibrium
was lacking.

The majority of such immigrants lacked patriotic
feelings. Of their former homeland oppressed under a
foreign yoke, they remembered only poverty. In America
also many were used as temporary labourers, who found employment in boom years and were thrown in the streets
during depressions.

Employers were mostly American-born; the Estonian
immigrants worked up at best to the position of foreman
or overseer. The social situation where the leading men
were American-born, the workers of other nationalities,
was such that the immigrants inevitably felt their inferiority.

The same factor existed in political life. The
majority of Estonians had not taken out American citizenship, and consequently had no vote. Political leaders
did not have to consider them, moreover they were few in
numbers. Their children who were born in America or were
young on arrival went to American schools. When the
parents could afford it, they sent their children to high
schools. Only a few went to universities.

But whatever else these children learned in schools,
they learned undeservedly to underrate their fathers'
homeland, and even their parents themselves, if these
clung to their Estonian nationality. The children changed
their names for English ones and became Americans...

A sudden change in the attitude of Estonian-Americans was brought about by the Estonian War of Liberation
in 1918-1920. The victorious conclusion of the war and
the establishment of the Estonian Republic helped to cure
this inferiority complex and raise their national pride.
Estonia was no longer the country of poor emigrants but
of victorious soldiers. Estonians in America suddenly
discovered with a certain pride that they were Estonians.
National reconstruction and the achievements at home, with
which the emigrants keep informed through participation
every five years in the Congress of Overseas Estonians,
have tended to increase this pride. Emigrants, revisit-
ing their homeland, find their country changed, and re-

turn to America with different views. A new spirit has
been developed by newer emigrants from independent Estonia, many of whom belong to the educated classes, who are
naturally more [ethnic] conscious than the earlier unskilled workers. And by now many of those earlier settlers have risen on the social ladder.

The Estonian language will disappear in America in a
couple of generations. The children learn only English
at school. This does not yet mean that these children
of Estonian parents who no longer speak Estonian have
lost all Estonian consciousness. Language is but one
element of nationality.

There are today in the U.S.A. many highly skilled
workers, merchants, and university professors of Estonian origin -- a situation of which it was impossible to
dream twenty-five to thirty years ago. Even in American
public life, there are Estonians who play a noteworthy
part.

The mental orientation of Estonians abroad is today
quite different from what it was before the World War and
the War of Liberation. Then Estonians who had been na-
turalized Americans knew no greater ambition than to become one hundred percent Americans. Theoretically they
are not allowed to feel any tie to their country of origin and in the oath taken on becoming an American citizen they have to relinquish all duties to another sovereign power and their former mother country. Yet there
is a change. Although the oath is the same, life has
silently given all new Americans the right to have a soft
spot for their old mother country and their old mother
tongue.

Estonians in the U.S.A. have today a new duty to
fulfill -- to be a bridge between two countries, to ac-
quaint Americans with Estonia and Estonians with America.

It would take us too far if we attempted to describe
conditions of Estonians in all continents and countries
where their numbers are smaller. Everywhere they are
organizing themselves on the same lines as in the U.S.A.
The only exceptions are the Estonians in the Soviet Union,
with whom every contact is lacking.

The overseas Estonian movement has its centre in
the Estonian Overseas Union -- a cultural society in Tallinn [the Estonian capital]. This is a private organization which, through the medium of a central office and
a periodical [Välis Eesti], keeps the overseas Estonian
societies in touch with one another and lends them cultural help. To the periodical congresses arranged by
the Union come Estonians from most countries and continents.

Document 5

THE UNITED STATES POSITION ON THE ANNEXATION
OF THE BALTIC STATES, 1940

When the Soviet Union occupied
and then forcibly annexed Estonia, Latvia and Lithuania in the
summer of 1940, most countries
did not accord legal recognition
to the move. The following press
release, issued in the name of
the Acting Secretary of State,
Sumner Welles, represented the
viewpoint of the American government.

Source: Archives of the Consulate General of the Republic of
Estonia (New York City).

July 23, 1940

Washington, D.C. (press release):

During these past few days the devious processes
whereunder the political independence and territorial
integrity of the three small Baltic republics — Estonia,
Latvia, and Lithuania -- were to be deliberately annihi-
lated by one of their more powerful neighbors, have been
rapidly drawing to their conclusion.

From the day when the peoples of these republics
first gained their independent and democratic form of
government the people of the United States have watched
their admirable progress in self-government with deep and
sympathetic interest.

The policy of this Government is universally known.
The people of the United States are opposed to predatory
activities no matter whether they are carried on by the
use of force or by the threat of force. They are likewise opposed to any form of intervention on the part of
one state, however powerful, in the domestic concerns of
any other sovereign state, however weak.

These principles constitute the very foundations upon which the existing relationship between the 21 sovereign republics of the New World rests.

The United States will continue to stand by these
principles, because of the conviction of the American
people that unless the doctrine in which these principles
are inherent once again governs the relations between nations, the rule of reason, of justice, and of law -- in

other words, the basis of modern civilization itself --
cannot be preserved.

Sumner Welles
Acting Secretary of State

Document 6

PROCLAMATION OF BALTIC STATES DAY IN NEW YORK, 1941

Herbert H. Lehman of New York was
the first governor of any state
to proclaim a Baltic States Day.
The original copy of the proclamation was reproduced in a New
York City Estonian monthly.

Source: Meie Tee (Our Path),
June, 1941.

May 28, 1941

The citizens of America, resolved to defend their
liberties at home and to champion the cause of representative government abroad, feel deep sympathy for the
peoples of those small republics whose independence
either has been crushed or is threatened.

Among those enslaved nations are the Republics of
Estonia, Latvia and Lithuania which have provided this
country with many loyal citizens now banded together in
the Baltic American Society to preserve the democracy
here and to restore its benefits in their home lands.

Estonia, Latvia and Lithuania have long been sym-
bols of liberty. Their people have for centuries made
great sacrifices for freedom and democracy. It is fitting, therefore, that the citizens of New York State
formally convey their sympathy to the people of these
enslaved nations and give public expression of the hope
that they will soon regain their freedom.

NOW, THEREFORE, I, Herbert H. Lehman, Governor of
the State of New York, do hereby designate Sunday, June
fifteenth, as BALTIC STATES DAY upon which appropriate
exercises may be held to celebrate the bonds of affection and regard existing between America and the distressed Baltic peoples.

/signed/
Herbert H. Lehman

Document 7

RESOLUTIONS ADOPTED BY THE BALTIC FREEDOM RALLY
IN NEW YORK CITY, 1941

> The following resolutions were
> adopted by the Baltic Freedom
> Rally, held in New York City's
> Town Hall on June 15, the day
> which the governor of the state
> had designated as Baltic States
> Day.
>
> Source: Archives of the Estonian
> Relief Committee, Inc. (New York).

WHEREAS, by the adoption of devious processes of
lying, treachery and chicanery erected into a Policy of
State, followed up by overwhelming military power in fur-
therance of predatory policies of communist aggression,
the Union of Soviet Socialist Republics has succeeded,
against the will of the populations, in establishing its
armed forces and administration in the territories of the
Republics of Estonia, Latvia and Lithuania; and

WHEREAS the communist authorities of occupation are
engaged in a deliberate and systematic depredation and
pillage of national wealth, industrial equipment, farm
produce and manpower of the invaded Baltic Nations and
mass transportation of the Estonian, Latvian and Lithuanian population into the interior of Russia, coupled
with expropriations, suppression of all civil and religious liberties, and extermination of intellectual and
labor leaders; and

WHEREAS the Government of the United States of
America, as well as the free peoples of other Democracies of the world, have not and never will recognize the
subjugation of the Baltic Republics by one of their more
powerful neighbors; and

WHEREAS the Governor of the State of New York by a
Proclamation, dated May 28th, 1941, has decreed and set
apart June 15th, the date of anniversary of Russian invasion, as BALTIC STATES DAY to formally convey the sympathy of the People of the State of New York to temporarily enslaved peoples of the Baltic Republics and to
give public expression of the hope that they will soon
regain their freedom;

Now, therefore,

BE IT RESOLVED, that we unequivocally concur in the policy of non-recognition of any Russian, German or other aggression in any form in any part of the world, consistently applied by our Government in steadfast adherence to the traditional American principles -- the rule of reason, of justice, and of law in international relations;

BE IT FURTHER RESOLVED, that we endorse the American policy of effective aid to the embattled British Commonwealth of Nations and other Democracies fighting for the restitution of a free association of independent states, including the Republics of Estonia, Latvia, and Lithuania;

BE IT FURTHER RESOLVED, that we gratefully join with our Honorable Governor's expression of sympathy, affection and regard for the distressed Baltic peoples and in the hope that they will soon regain their freedom;

BE IT FURTHER RESOLVED, that we protest most emphatically against the Soviet aggression and continuing occupation of the Baltic States, and that we respectfully urge our Government to sever relations with the faithless masters and oppressors of Russia; and

BE IT FINALLY RESOLVED, that copies of these resolutions be forwarded to the President and Secretary of State of the United States, the Governor of the State of New York, Members of Congress of the United States, the Embassy of Great Britain, the Legations of Estonia, Latvia and Lithuania, and the Mayor of the City of New York.

> DEN HOWE,
> CHAIRMAN, BALTIC FREEDOM RALLY.
>
> RICHARD HERMANSON,
> CHAIRMAN, BALTIC STATES DAY COMMITTEE.

BALTIC STATES DAY COMMITTEE
Chanin Building, Room 1220, New York City

Document   8

LETTER OF GRATITUDE RECEIVED BY THE WORLD ASSOCIATION OF
ESTONIANS FOR THE PURCHASE OF FIELD AMBULANCES FOR THE
UNITED STATES ARMY, 1944

> The Estonian-American community
> participated in the national war
> effort by the purchase of War
> Bonds. The money was used to
> purchase ambulances for the Army,
> and one ambulance operator sent
> the following letter to the World
> Association of Estonians.
>
> Source: Archives of the World As-
> sociation of Estonians, Inc. (New
> York City).

October 23, 1944
Somewhere in France

Gentlemen:

I wish to thank you for the Field Ambulance which
was presented by The World Association of Estonians to
the United States Army.

It is now in operation, and doing valiant service
under trying weather conditions. The purchase of War
Bonds reflect your patriotic interest in the welfare of
your country and those who are fighting to preserve it.

Again we wish to thank all Estonians for this kind
consideration. Our motto is: "To Conserve Fighting
Strength."

Sincerely yours,

Joseph T. Keady
"Operator"

Document 9

APPEAL OF AMERICANS OF ESTONIAN DESCENT
TO THE UNITED STATES CONGRESS, 1945

The following appeal was sent to
all members of Congress and also
to 1,600 newspaper editors, gov-
ernors, mayors, and university
presidents by the Estonian-American community. The full text was
reprinted in a New York Estonian
monthly.

Source: Meie Tee (Our Path),
April, 1945.

February 24, 1945

To Members of the Senate and the House
of Representatives of the United States:

We, Americans of Estonian descent, assembled on this
24th day of February, 1945, to commemorate the Declaration of Independence by the Estonian Republic in 1918,
respectfully submit the following facts, and enlist ur-
gent and definite action on your part as our representatives and lawmakers, in order to establish for the Estonian people their self-government as a sovereign democratic state "in accord with the freely expressed wishes
of the people concerned," as set forth in the principles
formulated in the Atlantic Charter.

We, Americans of Estonian descent, side by side with
fellow-citizens of the United States, have entered this
war in the spirit and with the avowed purpose of ending
tyranny everywhere in the world. Our sons, husbands, and
fathers are engaged in fighting on the seven seas, five
continents, and in the air -- performing all kinds of
tasks and holding ranks from private to that of colonel,
from able-bodied seamen to captain, from the Seabees to
the Merchant Marine. The graves in Africa, in the Pacific, in Europe and in Asia hold many of our honored dead --
dear ones who died in the belief that they were fighting
for the "Four Freedoms everywhere in the world" -- including Estonia. Our men and women are working throughout the nation -- in factories, shipyards, mines and mills
as laborers and highly skilled-technicians -- all making

their contribution in the effort for the elimination of
tyranny. We are paying taxes and producing weapons for
the same objective.

Much of our sweat and toil has gone into the food,
clothing, medical supplies and armaments which have been
shipped to Russia, and with them the Russians have been
able to clear their own land of the Nazi hordes.

But, ironically, part of this same supply of food,
clothing, medicine and material has been used by the
Russians for the destruction of the peoples of the Estonian Republic and of their independence. All in direct
violation of the United Nations Declaration, based upon
the principles of the Atlantic Charter (to which Russia
was a signatory). Deliberate annihilation, torture, mass
murder, mass exile and deportation by the Russians, have
taken place in Estonia. The beastliness and terror vis-
ited upon Estonia by the Russians have exceeded the record of every tyranny in history. Yet, all this has been
and continues to be perpetrated by an "ally" who has been
fed, clothed and equipped with supplies through our toil,
sweat and blood.

In the past we have appealed to our Administration,
through the White House and through the State Department.
We had hoped that at the Crimean Conference our government would take steps and assert itself in putting a
stop to the Russian atrocities against the peaceful free-
dom-loving and industrious nation of our ancestors; we
had hoped that our Administration would enforce the tenets
of the Atlantic Charter and thus rebuild the trust and
prestige of the United States in the eyes and hearts of
suffering mankind; that the Administration would make
clear to our Russian ally the fact that that which in-
creases the sum of human happiness is moral, and that
which diminishes the sum of human happiness is immoral;
and that slavery under the Germans, Japanese, or Russians
is not the friend of virtue.

We hold that an America strong enough and compas-
sionate enough to feed and to fight for the liberty of
the world, is not morally so weak and recreant to her
trust as to permit that the small peace-loving and democratic nations be sacrificed on the altar of death and
slavery, in order to make the world safe for the United
States, or to bring about the Four Freedoms everywhere
in the world. The voice of the great patriot, Patrick
Henry, again rings clear: "Is life so dear and peace so
sweet, to be bought at the price of chains and slavery?
Forbid it, Almighty God!"

The results of the Crimean Conference have brought
no change in the situation, at least so far as can be

gathered from published reports and radio announcements.
On the contrary, the Estonian people and their independence have been left to the mercy of the Russian tyranny. And no refuting statement has to date been forth-
coming from our public officials.

The destruction of Estonia, or any other peaceful
nation, is a crime, and we Americans of Estonian descent
do not want to become partners in this crime. Nor can
we ignore this treacherous act which sanctions the annihilation of peaceful nations, furthered and abetted by
the use of American supplies -- made, paid for and shipped by the people of the United States. To us such accord would rank equal with the worst known treachery in
civilized history. We do not want the blood of democratic peoples on our hands. It is not for this purpose
that we give our lives, our strength, and our tears. To
us, Estonian independence and freedom, and the security
and safety of our loved ones domiciled across the sea,
are as important as is the freedom, safety and sovereignty of the British, French or Belgian peoples, to the
Americans having origin in those roots.

The tyranny and suffering imposed upon the Estonian people, as well as the peoples of her neighboring
Baltic countries -- Lithuania and Latvia -- is terrify-
ing in the extreme, too long and horrible to set forth
in this letter. A more detailed account of it has been
sent to the State Department (in 1944); it ranges from
atrocious death by torture, to deportation and enslave-
ment of thousands. We, therefore, appeal to the United
States Congress, and request that a committee be formed
whose purpose it shall be:

1. To gather all available data concerning Russian conduct in Estonia and in other Baltic
   states from the materials and documents sub-
   mitted to the State Department by American
   Estonians, Latvians, and Lithuanians.

2. To dispatch a commission to neutral countries (such as Sweden), where refugees who
   have escaped from Estonia and other Baltic
   countries may be questioned in an effort to
   verify the accuracy of the situation.

And we respectfully request that the United States government take immediate steps for the re-establishment
of Estonian, Latvian, and Lithuanian full political and
territorial independence, in accordance with their own
freely expressed constitutional provisions existing be-

fore Russian occupation;   this to be effected under super-
vision of a joint American and British military commission.

THE ATLANTIC CHARTER
(A restatement of principles)

1. Their countries seek no aggrandizement, territorial
   or other.

2. They desire to see no territorial changes that do
   not accord with the freely expressed wishes of the
   peoples concerned.

3. They respect the right of all people to choose the
   form of government under which they will live; and
   they wish to see sovereign rights and self-government restored to those who have been forcibly de-
   prived of them.

4. They will endeavor, with due respect for their existing obligations, to further the enjoyment of
   all states, great or small, victor or vanquished,
   of access, on equal terms, to the trade and to the
   raw materials of the world which are needed for
   their economic prosperity.

5. They desire to bring about the fullest collabora-
   tion between all nations in the economic field
   with the object of securing, for all, improved
   labor standards, economic advancement and social
   security.

6. AFTER THE FINAL DESTRUCTION OF THE NAZI TYRANNY,
   THEY HOPE TO SEE ESTABLISHED A PEACE WHICH WILL
   AFFORD TO ALL NATIONS THE MEANS OF DWELLING IN
   SAFETY WITHIN THEIR OWN BOUNDARIES, AND WHICH
   WILL AFFORD ASSURANCE THAT ALL MEN IN ALL THE
   LANDS MAY LIVE OUT THEIR LIVES IN FREEDOM FROM
   WANT AND FEAR.

7. Such a peace should enable all men to traverse the
   high seas and oceans without hindrance.

8. They believe that all of the nations of the world,
   for realistic as well as spiritual reasons, must
   come to the abandonment of the use of force..."

These are the principles for which Americans of Estonian descent are fighting and dying. In the name of our

honored dead and those who will return, we entreat our public officials to enforce these principles where Estonia, Latvia, and Lithuania are concerned, as well as other liberated countries. We request that these principles be invoked now, at least to the extent that they have been invoked in Italy, Greece, France, and Belgium. We urge that the American-British Commission be appointed immediately to supervise the establishment of an orderly and constitutional government in Estonia, as also in Latvia and Lithuania. We exhort our Congress to exert every influence at its command to effect the return of Estonians who have been deported to Russia.

And borrowing the words of the Great Emancipator, Abraham Lincoln, we pray that ESTONIA "under God, shall have a new birth of freedom, and that government of the people, by the people, for the people, shall not perish from the earth."

Conrad Klemmer
Evangelical Lutheran Pastor

John Torpats
George Kukepuu
August Waldman
Committee for the Assembled

Document 10

CROSSING THE ATLANTIC OCEAN IN A 37-FOOT BOAT, 1945

> The following first-person account
> tells how some Estonians arrived in
> the United States after World War
> Two and why they came here.
>
> Source: Excerpt from "The Cruise
> of the Erma" by Voldemar Veedam
> with Carl B. Wall, The Reader's
> Digest, February, 1947. Copyright
> 1947 by the Reader's Digest Asso-
> ciation, Inc. Used with permission.

THE CRUISE OF THE ERMA

Stockholm, Sweden; July 5, 1945.

Maia Andre came to the house tonight with a letter
she had just received from the Swedish authorities. Her
hand trembled as she showed it to us. "It is the wish
of the government," the formal notice read, "that you
return to your home in Estonia..." The language is po-
lite, but the implication is frightening. It means that
Moscow is pressing to have us sent back to our homeland,
which is now under Soviet rule. Maia's letter is one
of many, I find, being mailed alphabetically to the Estonian political refugees who have fled across the Baltic in the past five years.
    In 1940 the U.S.S.R. took over our Republic of Es-
tonia. Hundreds fled to Finland and Sweden. In 1941
the Germans drove out the Russians. Thousands fled. In
1944 the Russians came back. Tens of thousands fled.
Today, of Estonia's one million population 30,000 are
here in Sweden, 60,000 roam the face of Europe, 60,000
are living or dead "somewhere in Russia."
    The Soviet [Union] now wants us to "come home..."
At the instigation of the Soviet [Union], the Swedish
State Police has conducted an official poll among Estonians here. Exactly 99.5 percent do not want to go home.
Why? It is fear. Fear of the NKVD, the Russian secret
police. Tonight Maia Andre's letter is not the only in-
dication that Moscow is thinking about us. There are
paid advertisements in the Stockholm newspapers asking
all Estonians to register at the Soviet Legation so that
we may be "returned to our homes."

"We can't just sit around here," Harry Paalberg
says. "Sooner or later we will be sent back. We must
do something. Let's get a boat and sail to America!"
"They will not let us in," Arvid Kuun objects. "We
have no visas."
"We will settle that when we get there," says Harry
confidently.
This is clearly a crazy idea -- but I'm for it.

Stockholm; July 8, 1945.

Harry has found a boat which we can afford to buy
and which he believes will carry us to America. Her name
is Erma. She is what the Swedes call a koster -- a sloop
built for coastal pleasure cruising. The owner claims
she is only 55 years old, but it is hard to tell...To me
Erma looks far too small. She is only 37 feet long...
Harry jabbed a penknife into Erma's planks as far below
the water line as he could reach...[The owner] said that
if we did not want to take her as she was, we could go
to hell. Harry believes the man is perfectly honest...

Göta Canal, Sweden; August 18, 1945.

These last weeks have been filled with backbreaking
work putting Erma in seagoing shape. We cleared Stockholm
nine days ago and we are now chugging at snail-pace toward the open sea. We chose this canal route because
the Russians are on the island of Bornholm, in the Baltic
between Sweden and Denmark, and there have been rumors
of strange disappearances in those waters...Originally,
Erma was a family pleasure boat designed to accomodate
four or five persons. There are 16 in our party, all
friends of happier days in Estonia...[The party includes
women, two aged 58 and 60, and four children, two of
them only three years old.]...In our aftercabin there is
also the engine -- an ancient one-cylinder auxiliary
which we installed after buying Erma...Harry and Arvid
are the only ones who have ever been to sea or know the
first thing about sailing a boat. Both, however, say they
are excellent navigators and "master mariners." I hope
they are not merely boasting...Erma must travel more than
7000 miles. Our supplies worry [Harry] a little. Since
it is unusual for Harry to worry about anything, this
worries the rest of us a good deal. The purchase of Erma
left us with very little cash. We have nine pint cans of
condensed milk for the children, six bags of potatoes,
three large bags of rice, some Swedish hard bread, oat-
meal, and a few cans of corned beef and sardines. We have
built water tanks into Erma's sides and lined them with
cement to retard souring. Harry says that, with very
strict rationing, there should be enough of everything

for 60 days.

Kragerö, Norway; August 26.

Four days ago we ran into a full gale in the blue green waters of the Skagerrak. Erma sprang a bad leak below the water line. In order to keep her from foundering in the heavy seas we had to man the pump constantly... One hundred strokes will pump 12-1/2 gallons. I made 500 such strokes each turn. So did every man on board. Still the water was within inches of the cabin floor boards. We decided to make for a Norwegian port...We hauled Erma up on a boatyard railway and had our first good look at her bottom. It was not good...termites had attacked her while hauled up on shore...It took most of what little money we had been saving for a real emergency but we managed to get a few copper sheets and some good paint... While the men were working, the women and children hiked to several coastal villages trying to buy more canned milk for the children. In three days they found two cans... We all stuck to speaking Swedish; we felt it safer. We left Sweden with official permission for a "cruise in coastal waters." The authorities may believe we are cruising too far.

North Sea; August 30.

We have quartered strong north-western winds for two days. Every five minutes, as though timed by some special device, a tremendous breaker crashes over Erma. The water trickles through the cabin roofs. Everything and everyone is soaked. Unfortunately, our seasickness is over. Unfortunately, because now we are hungry all the time...At dusk tonight we had something of a scare. I saw Arvid leap suddenly from the bow to the steering wheel. He spun it violently and we missed a floating mine by so little that I might have touched it. I do not know what nationality it was. Just another displaced item.

Loch Ness, Scotland; September 7.

...We are putt-putting through the Caledonian Canal system which connects the North Sea with the Atlantic. The immigration officials at Fraserburgh (being only human) seemed puzzled by our Estonian passports. Finally, with an air of "Oh, what the hell!" one of them stamped in the necessary visa. At the dock in Fraserburgh, I made the mistake of talking with a friendly man in a black hat. He was a newspaperman. The London Daily Mail carried a story referring to Erma as the "Mayflower of 1945."...The monks [at the Abbey of St. Benedictus in

Fort Augustus] gave us vegetables, fresh milk, candies
and cigarettes. We have been unable to buy further provisions. We spent our last money for some Diesel oil
which Harry says is now more important than food.

<u>Kingstown Bay, Ireland; September 24</u>.

Last night, while riding at anchor, <u>Erma</u> very nearly
met her end. A sudden equinoctial gale ripped across the
Irish Sea, tore her from anchorage and began driving her
toward rocky shoals which rim the harbor. There was only
one thing to do: start the auxiliary [motor] and hold
<u>Erma's</u> bow into the wind...Ahead in the blackness, through
the spume which whipped in solid sheets over the deck,
we could see the white fury of the water over the reefs.
We had drifted that close when the engine at last sput-
tered and turned over. Even with the auxiliary, Harry
could barely bring <u>Erma's</u> bow into the gale, but at last
we began to inch away from the reefs. All through the
night, however, one of us clung to the handle of the
pump and bobbed up and down for at least 500 strokes...

<u>Funchal, Madeira [Portugal]; October 10</u>.

...At one moment there was nothing, and then the
lovely green hills of Madeira rolled slowly up from the
horizon. Harry and Arvid, as co-captains, are the only
ones allowed ashore by the Portugese authorities. The
latter think we are, of all things, Communists! Estonia,
they say, is under Soviet domination. We have Estonian
passports. Ergo, we are Communists. Harry is cabling his
father in America for money. We are in desperate need of
fuel oil and supplies...

<u>At Sea; October 20</u>.

We left Madeira harbor in a dead calm today and
have already used ten gallons of our precious Diesel oil.
This leaves us with five gallons, which Harry says we
must save for running through the traffic of American
harbors. The money from Harry's father arrived after a
nine-day wait. We managed to buy some potatoes, rice,
bread, dried fish and a few cans of milk. But there was
not a pint of Diesel oil in Funchal...In Madeira Harry
and Arvid made very clear -- particularly to the women--
the dangers now before us. "We have lost precious time,"
Harry explained, "and we must weather bad storms before
we reach America." But we unanimously decided to go ahead.
As Mrs. Paalberg said: "It would be better to be drowned
than go back." Our next landfall, Harry says, will be
America, some 5000 miles from here as <u>Erma</u> sails, tack-
ing to catch the winds. He seems undecided whether we

should land at New York or Philadelphia.

At Sea; November 20.

    The last month has been like a vacation with pay in
Paradise. Like a happy duck, Erma has waddled on and on,
caressed by fair wind and blue seas...We talk a good deal
of what may lie ahead. Arvid, who has been to America as
a seaman, says that it is the one place left in the world
where he would like to raise his family. Harry says that
if the United States will not let us in without visas,
we will go on to South America. He even talks of Australia as another land of freedom and hope. Each morning Maia
has English classes for the four children. Their text is
an illustrated copy of Snow White and the Seven Dwarfs
which she bought in Scotland...In the afternoon, Harry
and Arvid shoot the sun with the sextant and compute our
position. We have no regular navigation charts, only a
large map of the Atlantic...Harry guesses our speed by
glancing at the water. Erma, he says, is a very steady
old lady. In this perfect weather she will do her four
knots -- no more, no less...

At Sea; December 4.

    Somehow we have weathered the [thunder] storm and
are now beating our way back slowly to the westward in
almost still air. We do not know where we are. When
Harry picked up the sextant this morning he found the
mirrored ruined. Paul has taken Ellen's pocket mirror
and is trying to cut it to fit the sextant. Erma has
taken a terrible beating. Last night the pump became
clogged with a potato which had washed into the bilge.
It took us two hours to get it working again. By that
time the floor boards were afloat. Harry fears one of
the copper patches has come loose! We ate the potato.
Because sharks are nuzzling the barnacles along Erma's
sides no one dares go overboard to inspect the damage.
Paul wanted to harpoon one with a spear he made in the
trade-winds area, but Harry says a shark would be twice
as dangerous in the boat as in the water...

At Sea; December 8.

    We are all suffering terribly from the cold. As
Heino says, we were properly dressed for a brisk walk in
the park but not for winter in the Atlantic...We are all
like wet sponges from the wave buffetings of the past
two days. When we lie down, the water squishes out in
streams. In the cabins, the women rub and slap the children. There is not a dry cloth on board with which to rub
them down. Their faces have a pinched, bluish look. Even
when they sleep they seem to shiver, but they cry only

at night when a particularly violent sea crashes over
us. Paul has finally succeeded in repairing the sextant.
We got a chance to shoot a fleeting, wintry sun, and
found that we were 350 miles east of Norfolk, Va. Today
is Lembit's 25th birthday. After his watch this afternoon, Maia and Ellen made their way over the slippery,
heaving deck to bring him a small can of Norwegian sardines which they heroically had saved for the occasion.
Maia had also written a poem which she read aloud...

At Sea; December 10.

...Harry says that the day after tomorrow we will
enter New York harbor We have had nothing but a cup of
rice apiece for days. The cement lining in the water
tanks has come loose, and our daily half cup is undoub-
tedly paving our stomach. But tonight it tastes good.

Midnight; December 12.

We were at a point only 50 miles off Atlantic City.
All we needed was another eight to ten hours of favor-
able winds. We didn't get them. Instead, another storm
broke over us. This time it howled straight out of the
north, a full gale. We tumbled helplessly southward
through the night. At times, giant combers roared over
the decks, flooded the helm cockpit. In the cabins
everything was afloat -- suitcases, shoes, bedding. The
children sensed the danger and cried pitifully...We were
now pumping at the rate of 1500 strokes in each four-
hour watch...

December 13.

The storm has died, and once more we are trying to
beat our way back to the west. Ice has formed on the
rigging. Even the pumping no longer gives us warmth. The
stoves have been wrecked by the storm, but the women
have a new invention: they pour a little alcohol on the
floor and light it. The children huddle around the flame.
Everything is so completely soaked there is no danger of
fire...Everyone seems exhausted. The children sleep most
of the time. We realize now that we are actually starv-
ing. What little drinking water is left must be strained
through a handkerchief and saved for the children. There
is some rice left, but our mouths are so dry we cannot
chew it. Even Harry now agrees that our only hope is to
be sighted by a passing ship.

December 14.

Harry was at the wheel and I was pumping when Ellen
came on deck. She stood for a moment looking wordlessly
out to sea, then pointed and screamed. We stared through
the falling snow, and saw a ship! It was bearing down on
us, a quarter mile away...Harry shouted, "She's seen us!
She's slowing down."...In a moment the ship came along-
side, and lines were dropped. Harry clambered up the
ship's ladder. Within ten minutes sailors began lowering
an avalanche of supplies: water, bread, hams, potatoes,
cans of coffee, cocoa and milk; bundles of clothing,
blankets, cigarettes; and Diesel oil for our engine...
As the ship pulled away we could read the name on her
stern, John P. Gray. She was a U.S. Navy auxiliary trans-
port...[Harry] had been given an armful of shore charts
by the Gray's captain. Now he happily spread them out on
the after-cabin roof and clapped Arvid on the back..."I
thought they would take us on board," [said Heino]. I
had been wondering about that myself...

December 15, [128 days after leaving Sweden]

We saw it for the first time in the blackness of
early morning. Arvid and Harry were in the helm cockpit.
Heino was at the pump. I had come up from below because
it was too cold to sleep. At first, it was a barely per-
ceptible glow along the western horizon. If it had been
to the east, it might have been merely the dawn. But it
was to the west and we knew that we were looking at the
light of America, reflected in the western sky. For some
time no one spoke...Of all of Europe's homeless, wander-
ing millions, we of the Erma were perhaps the most for-
tunate. In this new land, we would begin another life...
For the first time, Harry's voice sounded tight and
strained. "That would be Cape Henry," he said.

Long Island City, N.Y.; November 18, 1946.

For all of us, the voyage of Erma has had a happy
ending. A few weeks ago, President Truman intervened
with immigration authorities in behalf of Estonian political refugees. It now seems quite certain that we will
be given the privilege of eventually becoming citizens
of America. We all have jobs, though some may be small.
As Heino said the other evening, "I would rather scrub
floors in Brooklyn at $17.50 a week than make a million
within easy walking distance of the NKVD."

Document 11

NEWSPAPER EDITORIAL ON ESTONIAN REFUGEES, 1946

When Estonian refugees began to arrive
in the United States in late 1945 in
thirty and forty-foot boats without immigration visas, the immigration authorities threatened to deport them. The
following is an example of the many edi-
torials which American newspapers wrote
on the matter.

Source: Philadelphia Record, September
11, 1946.

WILL MAYFLOWER DESCENDANTS FIGHT FOR NEW PILGRIMS?

We would like to see a national movement to demand
admission for two groups of 1946 Pilgrims who have beaten
their way to this country in tiny fishing sloops.

We would like to see the movement led by the Society
of Mayflower Descendants.

The present-day Pilgrims are Estonians. The first
group of 18 landed August 21 in Miami, Florida. Eleven
more reached the same port Monday.

By strange coincidence, the Society of Mayflower
Descendants on Monday opened its first general congress
since the war at Plymouth, Mass. -- where the Mayflower
reached port 326 years ago.

The men and women and children on the Mayflower were
seeking religious freedom. The men and women and children from Estonia are seeking political freedom.

The Pilgrims of 1620 couldn't stand the persecutions
under King James. The Estonians can't stand the persecutions under Stalin.

Capt. Felix Tandre, skipper of the first Estonian
ship, the Inarda, talks in language reminiscent of the
founders of this country.

Gov. William Bradford referred to the early colonists as "pilgrims and strangers upon the earth."

Capt. Tandre says: "If we must go on, we will, even
if we must travel all the way to Australia. Our ship is
small, but it has taken us this far. They can't take the
sea away from us."

The colonists on the Mayflower signed the agreement
that became famous as the Mayflower Compact "for our better ordering and preservation."

Capt. Tandre says the Estonians chose the U.S. "because there was no other land which offered such freedom and security, where one can peacefully build a home and be sure no one can take it from him."

There was no liberty, he said, in his native land under either the Germans or the Russian "liberators." There was, he said, "no choice between those two."

The Pilgrims were met by unfriendly Indians.

The 1946 seekers after freedom have been met by immigration inspectors who have so far refused them entry.

Technical reason for refusing entry to the Estonians is that the quota of their country -- 116 a year -- has been exhausted.

That's a bit of hypocritical red tape.

We technically recognize Estonia as an independent nation.

But our Government has done nothing to prevent Russia incorporating Estonia and the other Baltic States into the Soviet Union. Not many refugees are able to escape from Russia proper. Maybe we should play the Russian game temporarily and admit the Estonians under the Russian quota.

But in any case we must let them in.

They're the kind of people we want -- willing to risk their lives for freedom. They set sail in 38-foot sloops. The Mayflower was 90 feet long. One of Columbus' vessels was 163 feet long.

They didn't wait until somebody sent them first-class steamship tickets. They came under their own power.

When they got here, they didn't try to enter in defiance of the law or by subterfuge. They identified themselves and asked for permission to enter.

They turned down offers of charity. All they asked was a chance to go to work.

Let's give these modern refugees from tyranny a chance at freedom -- a freedom we can't guarantee them in their own country. Let's prove we can recognize a 1946 version of the Pilgrim spirit.

And we'd like to see the meeting at Plymouth this week come to the defense of the Estonians, and spend less time debating a museum of early colonial life.

Document 12

STATEMENT OF SENATOR LEHMAN OF NEW YORK, 1951

Between 1945 and 1951 a number of small boats carrying Estonian refugees arrived in the United States from Sweden. When immigration authorities threatened to deport them because they arrived without visas, Senator Lehman of New York led a successful Congressional effort to enact special legislation allowing the refugees to remain in the country. Senator Lehman issued the following statement on the occasion.

Source: Archives of the Estonian Relief Committee, Inc. (New York City).

September 11, 1951

I am today introducing a bill to provide asylum in this country for 84 individuals now in the United States who, in 1948 and 1949, fled from tyranny in Estonia, their native land.

These individuals came to this country by way of Sweden. They came in three groups, in small open boats, across the North Atlantic, preferring the rigors of the open sea to Soviet rule and oppression. At the time of their arrival, there were many newspaper accounts of the dangers and hardships which these individuals had faced and overcome to get to our shores. Storm and sea were only the first of the hazards of this flight to freedom.

Shortly after the arrival of these groups in the United States, President Truman, exercising his emergency authority, granted them temporary asylum pending disposition of their cases in the Congress. Last year Congress considered a measure to grant permanent residence to these people. That bill was not acted upon. Now these Estonians are faced with deportation -- deportation to certain death -- or what might be worse than death -- the concentration and slave-labor camps of Siberia.

These individuals came to this country directly from Sweden. They can of course be deported to that country. Sweden has, unfortunately, accepted as a legal fact the violent incorporation of Estonia into the Soviet Union. Hence, under the laws of Sweden, these

people are Soviet subjects and would be deported from
Sweden, back to their native land and, as I have said,
to death, persecution or imprisonment.

Our Immigration and Naturalization Service has now
issued deportation orders for these people. I hope
that the Senate will speedily consider and approve my
bill which will permit these men, women and children,
after proper screening, to remain in this country.
After escaping from behind the Iron Curtain and after
heroically overcoming the hazards of the North Atlantic
in their small motor and sail ships, these refugees
from tyranny should certainly be given harbor and haven
in this country. That gesture on our part would be
well understood the world over, especially behind the
Iron Curtain. We would thus provide a happy ending to
this flight from terror, to this break from the Soviet
prison-house.

I do not know these individuals personally or in-
dividually, nor do I know their exact political or intellectual orientation. They have, indeed, been vouch-
ed for by reputable American organizations. I know one
thing, that these people were seeking freedom and were
trying to escape from oppression. America meant to
these individuals -- as it has always meant to all the
peoples of the world -- the land of freedom. Let it
ever remain so. Let us show the great heart of America,
and the hospitality of America, and the meaning of
America as the homeland of freedom, by giving prompt
and sympathetic consideration to this bill.

Herbert H. Lehman

Document 13

LETTER ANNOUNCING THE FORMATION OF THE
ESTONIAN WORLD COUNCIL, 1954

The following letter of introduction of the Estonian World Council
gives an overview of the goals and
purposes of the New York-based international organization.

Source: Archives of the Estonian
World Council (New York City).

Gentlemen:

This is to announce that the central organization
of the Estonians in the free world, the "Estonian World
Council," has started its activities.

The "Estonian World Council" is formed of the representatives of the Estonian central organizations in all
the countries of the free world where larger groups of
Estonians are living, namely, in the U.S.A., Canada,
Great Britain, Sweden, German Federal Republic and Australia.

The structure of the various central organizations
represented in the "Estonian World Council" differs in
detail. But the general underlying principle of these
organizations is that, they consist 1) of directly elected representatives of Estonians or the league of Estonian organizations [in the] respective countries and 2)
of former members of the Estonian Parliament and Government. Thus, at least 90 per cent of Estonians in the
free world are represented in the "Estonian World Council."

The principal aim for the establishment of this
council was to coordinate the efforts of the Estonians
in fighting communism and in their endeavours for li-
berating the nations behind the Iron Curtain.

Taking up our activities, we will be happy to col-
laborate with you, and we trust that a close coordination of all anti-Communist forces will be decidedly in
the interest of our common cause.

Respectfully
JUHAN VASAR, Chairman

Document 14

LETTER FROM FORMER PRESIDENT EISENHOWER TO ESTONIAN VETERANS, 1968

In 1968 Estonian-Americans observ-
ed the fiftieth anniversary of the
declaration of independence of the
Republic of Estonia, the country
of their origin, and of the beginning of the Estonian War of Independence. Estonian veterans in
the United States received the following letter from Dwight D. Eisenhower, thirty-fourth president of
the United States.

Source: Archives of the Legion of
Estonian Liberation, Inc. (New
York City).

February 2, 1968

I send greetings and best wishes to the veterans
celebrating the 50th Anniversary of the Estonian Independence War.

I am confident that the goals and efforts of the
people of your nation will renew in all citizens a determination to show the patriotic spirit displayed during your struggle against a common enemy.

/signed/
Dwight D. Eisenhower

Document 15

OVERVIEW OF THE ESTONIAN-AMERICAN COMMUNITY
OF LAKEWOOD, NEW JERSEY, 1973

The following excerpt is from an
article entitled "Estonian-American Community Importance to Lakewood Is Stressed," by Aleksander
Prima, Einar Pustrõm, and Juhan
Simonson in a local newspaper.

Source: Excerpted with permission
from the Ocean County Daily Times
(Lakewood, New Jersey), August 3,
1973.

    During the last several decades, the name Lakewood
has become literally a household word to a segment of
the residents of such far-flung places as Los Angeles,
Calif., Toronto, Canada and Stockholm, Sweden.
    Frequent reference is made to Lakewood on the Voice
of America facilities beaming broadcasts to EASTERN Europe. An occasional traveler boarding plane in Sidney,
Australia is likely to include Lakewood as a stopover on
his world itinerary.
    Such wide-scale awareness of our fair Township is
to a considerable measure attributable to the existence
of a rather small, yet extremely active community of
Estonians, who over the years, have settled in Lakewood
and its environs...
    Closer to home the Estonian-Americans are also
known to many of the Shore Area residents, who have read
from local newspapers about the frequent activities
sponsored by the Estonian organizations in the Lakewood
area, or who have even had opportunity to attend some
of these affairs themselves. Many others have formed
close personal associations with the newcomers to this
area through professional, business or social contacts.

    In the early 1930's several Estonian families pur-
chased land in the Lakewood-Jackson area and settled
here. As far as it is known, the first Estonian family
to settle here was the Lacht family. This was in 1933.
About the same time John Noop and his family established
a home here. Some other families to establish early re-
sidency in the area included Kaiv and Markus, Estonian
diplomats, and Mannapsoo, Part, Pruun, Enno, Kelman, and
others. If ever a community can claim that it got its
beginnings from a nest of eggs, the Lakewood Estonian-
American community can surely claim such a distinction.

For early Estonians, with few exceptions, were egg farmers as were most of their American neighbors and friends.
    Many Estonians from New York City began to visit
their friends who had settled in the Lakewood-Jackson
area. They spent weekends, then summers, and gradually
purchased land and began to settle here. The New York
born Virve Pustrom, the present president of the Lakewood Estonian Association, recalls that "as a child in
the 1930's my memories of Lakewood were tied into a summer package containing anticipation, excitement, fun,
a ferry ride from Fulton Street to the train terminal in
New Jersey, a long train ride down the coast and the
pines, which signalled one's arrival in Lakewood." She
also later became a resident of the Shore area.
    As with most ethnic communities, a desire to draw
together, perpetuate its culture, language, national
holidays and traditions took root among these early Estonian settlers. This was satisfied at first by gathering in each others homes, later in hired rooms and rent-
ed halls, mainly the "Maennerchoir," a German Club. However, the desire to have their own clubhouse where Estonians would find a community home grew.
    In 1945 a group of 28 Estonians got together and
formed the beginnings of the Lakewood Estonian Association. They adopted a constitution and elected officers.
    The late Konstantin Lacht donated a piece of land
adjoining his property at Cross Street and New Egypt
Road, just outside the Lakewood boundary in Jackson Township and plans for a clubhouse were formed. In 1946 the
association was incorporated and construction started.
By June, 1947, the first function, a centuries old traditional mid-summer night festival "Jaanipaev,"was held
at the Estonians own clubhouse. The first building was
a rather modest 30 foot by 80 foot hall designed mainly for social events with a small dining area, bar and
kitchen at the basement level. The membership of the
association had already grown to about 60...
    In 1949 and 1950 a great influx of Estonian immi-
grants to the United States began arriving mainly from
the refugee camps in war-torn Germany. A number of Estonian families settled here in the Lakewood area, mainly because the earlier settlers were willing and able to
become sponsors to the newcomers thus guaranteeing them
work and a place to stay in their adopted homeland...

    From the small beginning in the 1930's the Estoni-
an-American community in this area has been growing
steadily and has now three main organizations: The Lakewood Estonian Association, Inc., the Estonian Evangelical
Lutheran Holy Ghost Church, and the Federation of Associations for the Advancement of Estonian Youth, Inc....

    At present time, the association owns fully equip-

ped facilities for social gatherings, lectures, art
shows, and theatre performances. The indoor seating capacity is about 300 persons...

The association owns about 7.7 acres of land, about
half of it is still in a natural state, covered with
trees and shrubs. Since the Estonians hail from a country where forests and natural beauty abound, they have
always been "ecology-minded" and will continue to strive
to blend their homes and club facilities with the nature.

In 1957, a sharpshooting range was built on the Association's grounds. This building has a 50 meter shooting range in accordance with national laws and rules.
Numerous matches between Estonian sharpshooters and also
local and East Coast American units have been held here.
In 1971 during an international sharpshooting match the
world record for indoor shooting was broken here...

There is also a separate sauna building on the clubhouse property. The sauna has been a centuries long traditional way for Estonians to clean and invigorate ones
body, and is therefore a must to any Estonian Club...

There is also an outdoor stage and arena with a
seating capacity of about 2,000 [for] large gatherings
and summer festivals. Due to the availability of such
a large facility, the Lakewood Estonian Association has
been able to sponsor large-scale song and sports festivals filling the outdoor arena to capacity. The outdoor
stage area also doubles as a volleyball and basketball
court and has been subjected to intensive use... All im-
provements and additional buildings have been paid for
by the association solely from donations of its membership. These donations have been either cash donations
or in the form of materials and labor. No funds have
been received from any outside source.

The Estonian House has been for years a favored
gathering place of Estonian-Americans for the East Coast
and even Canada. During the summer months, three major
outdoor festivals are usually held. The first of these
is the mid-summer night festival... It takes place on
the shortest night of the year and the legend has that
on this night the "Twilight" and "Dawn" meet and kiss
for a brief moment only to part again and to wait another year. On this enchanted night also the fern is
supposed to bloom. The young will search for its flower
and whoever finds it will be blessed with happiness for-
ever...

The first weekend in August brings to Lakewood-
Jackson area Estonian athletes from all over the United
States and Canada to compete in the annual Sports Fes-
tival. The Estonians have always put great emphasis on
sports and physical fitness and their descendants in the
Free World are carrying on this tradition. This year

marks the nineteenth Sports Festival of the East Coast.
A few years ago, the world famous girl gymnasts from
Sweden, the Malmoflickornas, performed here under the
leadership of Mrs. Leesment, an Estonian who resides now
in Sweden. Also a special feature of the Sports Festival are volleyball matches, a popular sport of the Estonians. The Estonian Athletic Union in USA, Inc. orga-
nizes and arranges sports festivals and meets here and
in other parts of the country...

The Lakewood Estonian Association has also been
host to two Song Festivals where the late Valdeko Loigu
of Lakewood was the chairman and one of the conductors
of male, mixed and women choruses from throughout the
United States and Canada...

The third outdoor festival is a two-day celebration
on the Labor Day weekend,which [as] the Sports Festival
and Mid-summer Night Festival, provides an outdoor show
under lights where top Estonian-American entertainers
and folk dance groups perform. In addition on the Labor
Day weekend an extensive outdoor art show usually takes
place where Estonian artists from the United States and
Canada exhibit their work. Many of the paintings on display at these exhibits have found a cherished place in
the homes of shore residents.

During the winter season numerous cultural, social
and educational activities take place at the Estonian
House. A number of concerts, twice by the male chorus
from Stockholm, Sweden and on several occasions by
choruses from Canada have been given on the stage of[the]
Estonian House. The association also sponsors numerous
indoor art shows, lectures on various topics of interest,
book exhibits, etc.

The Legion of Estonian Liberation [an organization
of Estonian veterans] has its local chapter in the Estonian Club. On several occasions the veterans have had
their national conventions and other events in Lakewood.
The Lakewood Chapter has placed a memorial for fallen
national heroes at the Woodlawn Cemetery... The Estonian
veterans have developed close relationship with the American Legion Post in Lakewood and often participate in
each others activities.

The members of the fairer sex in the Estonian-American community have formed the Lakewood Estonian Women's
Club, which is a member of the nationally established
Federation of Estonian Women's Clubs. The Lakewood
Women's Club has two main objectives -- to promote Estonian culture and heritage and to raise funds for the
beautification of the clubhouse. The Women's Club has organized numerous handicraft exhibits in New Jersey libraries, including two month-long displays at the Lakewood
Public Library. They have also donated English-language
books about Estonia to several libraries and schools...

Half of the charter members of the Lakewood Estonian Association were women and two of the association presidents have been of the female gender, Vaike Kiin in the 1960's and the present Virve Pustrom.

During the winter, the Estonian Club houses the Estonian School, which meets every other Saturday morning. The objective of the school is to teach the youngsters of Estonian parentage the Estonian language, history, geography, literature and other subjects related to their heritage. The school has about 40 pupils from 6-15 years of age...

The Estonian Boy Scout Troop 12 has been for years one of the leading units in Ocean County. From 1955 to 1972 there have been ten promotions to the rank of Eagle Scout. In the Leo Paabo family, all four sons have achieved that rank -- a truly remarkable achievement. The Estonians also have an organized Girl Scout unit...

Our Folk Dance group under the direction of Ferdinand Rikka has been active since the early 1950's... The group has become well known on the East Coast [and it has] performed at the New York World's Fair, the Philadelphia Folk Fair, at several festivals in New York and Trenton, the Estonian World Festival in Toronto, Canada, and just this past June at the mammoth first Baltic-American Festival in the Garden State Arts Center...

To provide its youngsters with meaningful activities has always been a major concern of the Lakewood Estonian Association... Therefore a group of parents and youngsters got together to convert a less-used portion of the clubhouse exclusively for the use of our teenagers. This area consists of four separate units. It has a living room type area with sofas and chairs, a TV and juke box. Then there is a play area with a ping-pong table and hopefully soon a billiard table. There is a fully equipped kitchen and another room where the youngsters can hold their meetings. The activities are under the direction of Irene Verder, Eda Treumuth and Einar Pustrom, MD. This teen room has become popular with the youngsters, particularly since most of the renovations were done by them. They take real pride in keeping the area in good condition. For the fall, a program of lectures, movies, field trips, career days and talent shows will be presented...

The Lakewood Estonian Theatre has been active almost from the inception of the association. The repertoire is mostly Estonian. However, plays by Finnish and German authors have also been performed. The performances, which are in the Estonian language, have included dramas, comedies and musicals. The performances are always well attended and are most popular...

The theatre has given performances in New York
City, Baltimore, Connecticut, Long Island and Toronto...
At the First Estonian World Festival in the summer of
1972 in Toronto, over 3,000 Estonians enjoyed an original musical by Lembit Koorits called "High Society,"
which delightfully spoofs many aspects of Estonian life
abroad. Most of the actors and actresses are amateurs,
although there are a few who received their theatrical
training in Estonian drama school and the Estonian stage.
The theatre is under the direction of Leida Lepik, a
well known actress of Estonia. Last year the theatre
announced and organized a worldwide playwrights contest
in order to enrich the repertoire of original Estonian
language plays. This contest drew a total of 22 plays...

In 1948, an Estonian Evangelical Lutheran congregation was established in Lakewood. The first church service was held by Rev. Max E. Saar on Nov. 28 of that
year at the Immanuel Lutheran Church, Central Avenue,
Lakewood... Due to the growth needs of the congregation,
plans for a new church were made and property for this
purpose was acquired on East Seventh Street, near the
Lakewood High School. The construction of the new
church building was truly an Estonian community under-
taking. Hundreds of congregation members donated count-
less hours of labor, materials and money, during a one
year period of construction.
The first service was held at the new modern church
on June 2, 1964, by the Rev. Rudolf Reinaru. The dedi-
cation was Aug. 30, 1964. The Rev. Mr. Reinaru had become the minister of the Estonian Evangelical Lutheran
Holy Ghost Church in 1957 and has served the church
since then. The church seats approximately 250 persons...
The church building, for which no outside funds were received, has been fully paid for. Last year the congregation commissioned an altar painting by the well known
Estonian artist Endel Koks of Sweden. This huge painting measuring 16 feet by 11 feet was blessed and dedicated in a special service April 9, 1973 by Estonian
Archbishop Konrad Veem of Sweden... Three tall hand-
hewed wood crosses standing   near the church main en-
trance, constitute a unique landmark in church architecture in Lakewood...

Another major Estonian organization whose activities and facilities center in Lakewood and vicinity is
the Federation of Associations for the Advancement of
Estonian Youth, Inc. This organization was established
in late 1953 in Lakewood for the purpose of purchasing,
managing and maintaining a site for camping and other
outdoor activities for Estonian youth and scout groups.
The first segment for a campsite was acquired in 1955
in the Bennetts Mills area of Jackson Township. It com-

prised approximately 22 acres of former cranberry bogs
and wooded area. Later purchases have expanded the total
campsite area to about 88 acres. A number of needed
buildings and facilities have been constructed on the
site, including a year round administration and communication building, a kitchen and dining hall, a sauna,
restrooms, nature trails and a lake for swimming. All
facilities were built by volunteer community effort...
     The camping season held mostly in August, usually
lasts 10 to 14 days. However, the facilities are used
for training and educational purposes at other times of
the year, even by adults. The biggest event at the campsite took place in the summer of 1967 when the Federation was host to the worldwide Estonian Scouts Jamboree,
which attracted approximately 1,000 Estonian youths from
U.S.A., Canada, Sweden, Germany, Argentina, Australia
and other parts of the world...

* * * *

     When the Estonian refugees arrived in the shore area,
their first task was to begin building new lives for themselves and their families. Regardless of their background,
education and experience, the newcomers had to accept
whatever means of employment were available, at the time
this being mainly poultry farming and the building trade...
Through hard work and persistence, the newcomers soon established themselves in the community and began making
significant contributions to the local economy. Numerous
contracting and building firms with strange sounding Estonian names sprung up in the Lakewood area...
     After the Estonians had secured themselves in their
field of employment and established their own homes,
they began to get involved in local charitable, professional, political, and social fields. In the construction
field, many became members of the New Jersey Shore Build-
ers Association, and some, like Anton Mannik and Harry
Must, have been board members at various times. During
the Paul Kimball Hospital Fund Drive, the Estonian-American community, coordinated by Aino Piirsalu actively
participated in the drive...
     In the Township affairs, Harry Must has been a
member of the Mayor's Traffic Coordinating Committee and
Aleksander Prima is a member of the Township's Environ-
mental Commission. The Lakewood Estonian community has
enthusiastically participated in the Lakewood Summer
Festival and has, in fact, won several awards for these
efforts... In the last election, Anne Treumuth was elected a member of the Jackson Township Committee. Members
of both political parties have found a welcome in the Estonian Club, and many have used the forum to address
gatherings. Congressman James J. Howard, State Senator
John F. Brown, and the Mayors of both Lakewood and Jackson have been guests of the Estonian community...

The younger generation of Estonian-Americans, most
of whom come from "two language" homes have performed
well in schools and academic pursuits and have broken
many of the area's sports records. Many Estonian-American students have been high school cheerleaders, color-
guard captains and members of the band. Young Estonians, Malle Mandel, Ulle Viiroja, Peeter Feldman and
Rein Haus [were high school valedictorians]...

The local Estonian community is also making significant contributions to the Estonian organizations
and affairs at the national level. The Lakewood folk
dancers and athletes have participated in all major Estonian festivals and meets on the East Coast and Canada. The local veterans have attended national conventions, and Estonian school teachers have participated
in educational seminars in New York and Toronto.

Olev Piirsalu, a Lakewood resident, is a former
president of the Estonian World Council, and the late
Julius Kangur was the president of the Estonian American National Council. Presently Harry Must and Juhan
Simonson are vice-presidents of this national organization, and two other area residents, Heinz Riivald and
Harry Verder are members of the Board of Directors...

The ultimate goal of the association and its
members is to help in whatever manner they can to restore independence and freedom in Estonia.

Document   16

CONGRESSIONAL CONCURRENT RESOLUTION, 1973

In 1973 the House of Representatives
referred to the Committee on Foreign
Affairs the following concurrent resolution introduced by Congressman
Derwinski of Illinois.

Source: Archives of the Estonian
American National Council (New York
City).

December 5, 1973

Whereas the three Baltic nations of Estonia, Latvia, and
    Lithuania have been illegally occupied by the Soviet
    Union since World War II; and

Whereas the Soviet Union will attempt to obtain the re-
    cognition by the European Security Conference of its
    annexation of these nations; and

Whereas the United States delegation to the European Se-
    curity Conference should not agree to the recogni-
    tion of the forcible conquest of these nations by
    the Soviet Union:

Now, therefore, be it

    Resolved by the House of Representatives (the
Senate concurring), That it is the sense of the
Congress that the United States delegation to the
European Security Conference should not agree to
the recognition by the European Security Conference
of the Soviet Union's annexation of Estonia, Latvia
and Lithuania and it should remain the policy of the
United States not to recognize in any way the annexation of the Baltic nations by the Soviet Union.

Document 17

LETTER FROM SECRETARY OF STATE KISSINGER TO
CONSUL GENERAL JAAKSON, 1974

The United States, as well as
most other Western countries,
have never legally recognized
the Soviet annexation of Estonia in 1940. The continuation
of this policy is reflected in
the following letter received
by Ernst Jaakson, Consul General of the Republic of Estonia
in Charge of Legation.

Source: Archives of the Consulate General of the Republic
of Estonia (New York City).

February 19, 1974

On the occasion of the fifty-sixth anniversary of
the proclamation of Estonian independence, I am pleased
to extend to you and to the Estonian people greetings and
best wishes on behalf of the Government and people of the
United States of America.

This anniversary underscores the efforts of the Estonian people to maintain their cultural heritage and to
secure an independent national life in their homeland.
Their continuing pursuit of these goals has won the respect and admiration of the American people and of people
everywhere who **value** courage and freedom.

/signed/
Henry A. Kissinger

Document 18

NEW JERSEY GENERAL ASSEMBLY RESOLUTION,   1974

> In 1974 the Estonian-American com-
> munity of Seabrook, New Jersey,
> celebrated its twenty-fifth anni-
> versary. The New Jersey General
> Assembly adopted the following re-
> solution on the occasion.
>
> Source: Archives of the Estonian
> Association at Seabrook, New Jersey.

May 16, 1974

WHEREAS, The Estonian-American community at Seabrook, New
Jersey, Cumberland County, will observe its 25th Anniversary on Saturday, May 25, 1974; and

WHEREAS, It was in the Spring of 1949 when the first Estonian refugees from the displaced persons camps in
Western Germany began arriving at Seabrook, New Jersey, sponsored by the late Charles F. Seabrook; and,

WHEREAS, Two ministers of the Estonian Lutheran Church at
Seabrook have had the honor of offering the opening
prayer in the U.S. Senate and House of Representatives in Washington, D.C.; and,

WHEREAS, Several Estonian youths have achieved the distinction of being class valedictorians at the Bridge-
ton High School, and a number of former residents of
Seabrook have achieved doctorate degrees at various
universities throughout the country; and,

WHEREAS, Over the past quarter of a century, the Estonian-
Americans have made significant contributions to the
cultural and economic sphere of the local community,
Cumberland County and in southern New Jersey;

NOW, THEREFORE, Be It Resolved, That the General Assembly of the State of New Jersey mark May 25, 1974, as
a significant milestone in the development of this unique
community, and offers its wholehearted congratulations to

Mr. Albert Vilms, President of the Estonian Association
at Seabrook, all Estonian-Americans who live in Seabrook
or who reside in other parts of the United States; and,

Be It Further Resolved, That an authenticated copy
of this resolution, signed by the Speaker and attested
to by the Clerk of the New Jersey General Assembly, be
forwarded to Mr. Albert Vilms.

/signed/   /signed/
John J. Miller   S. Howard Woodson
Clerk   Speaker

Document 19

LETTER FROM GOVERNOR MANDEL TO MARYLAND
ESTONIANS, 1974

On September 21, 1974, the Baltimore
Estonian-American community celebrated the tenth anniversary of its
Estonian House. The governor of the
state sent the following letter on
the occasion.

Source: Archives of the Baltimore
Estonian Society, Inc.

September 1974

I welcome the opportunity to extend greetings to
all Marylanders of Estonian heritage as you celebrate
the 10th Anniversary of the Baltimore Estonian House.

And on this special occasion, I especially want to
salute your efforts to preserve the rich historical
heritage and unique culture of your homeland.

Through the many civic-minded activities in which
you have participated, you have contributed significant-
ly to the betterment of our State, and I extend to you
my best wishes that the Baltimore Estonian House will
continue to grow and to prosper in the coming years.

/signed/
Marvin Mandel

Document 20

BALTIMORE CITY COUNCIL RESOLUTION ON THE ESTONIAN
WORLD FESTIVAL OF 1976

> In 1976 the Baltimore Estonian-
> American community will host the
> Estonian World Festival, which
> is expected to attract about
> 20,000 Estonians from around the
> world. The Baltimore City Coun-
> cil adopted the following reso-
> lution in regard to the festival
> in 1973.
>
> Source: Archives of the Estonian
> Salute to Bicentennial '76, Inc.
> (Baltimore).

BILL NO. 966, CITY COUNCIL OF BALTIMORE

Walter S. Orlinsky, President and Members of the
City Council introduced July 9, 1973, read and adopted
A Bill Entitled City Council Resolution Inviting the
Estonian International Convention to hold their 1976
Convention in Baltimore and to designate the week of
July 5 -- July 11, 1976, as "Estonian Salute to Bicen-
tennial Week."

WHEREAS, during the year 1976, the two hundredth anniversary of the Declaration of Independence of the American colonies will be celebrated in the City of Baltimore, State of Maryland, as well as throughout the United
States of America, and

WHEREAS, it is fitting that persons of diverse national
and cultural background and heritage participate in the
bicentennial celebration commemorating American independence as they shared the burdens of the War of Independence and contributed, throughout two centuries, to the
growth of the independent American states, and

WHEREAS, citizens of Baltimore City of Estonian heritage
desire to commemorate the bicentennial celebration by
sponsoring in Baltimore City from July 5 through July 11,
1976, a convention for expatriate Estonians throughout
the world, and

WHEREAS, the Mayor and City Council of Baltimore wish to
welcome to Baltimore City all persons from throughout

the world who will participate in the said convention and to assist in making it a successful and memorable event as part of a program to commemorate the bicentennial of American independence.

NOW, THEREFORE, it is, by the Mayor and City Council of Baltimore, hereby

RESOLVED, that the week of July 5 through July 11, 1976, be and it is hereby designated as "Estonian Salute to Bicentennial '76 Week," and

FURTHER RESOLVED, that persons of Estonian heritage from throughout the world be and they are hereby invited to hold an international convention during the said week in Baltimore City as part of its commemoration in 1976 of American independence, and

FURTHER RESOLVED, that the said Mayor and City Council of Baltimore City shall make, and cause to be made, available facilities required for the said convention on terms comparable to those which shall be extended to other persons and groups of persons who shall take part in events and activities commemorating in 1976 in Baltimore City the bicentennial of American independence.

APPENDIX

Table 1

IMMIGRATION FROM ESTONIA TO THE UNITED STATES
1923 - 1957

Source: Unpublished study of
Estonian immigration by Tõnu
Parming, University of Maryland.

Year	Number		Year	Number
1923	241		1940	99
1924	775		1941	70
			1942	28
1925	158		1943	21
1926	158		1944	28
1927	166			
1928	168		1945	19
1929	166		1946	136
			1947	184
1930	159		1948	225
1931	125		1949	1840
1932	54			
1933	unknown		1950	5422
1934	105		1951	2073
			1952	1248
1935	72		1953	158
1936	102		1954	228
1937	92			
1938	124		1955	229
1939	192		1956	469
			1957	440

These figures show the immigration of persons born in Estonia.
Excluded are Estonians born in
other countries.

Table   2

NUMBER OF ESTONIANS ACQUIRING AMERICAN CITIZENSHIP
1938 - 1968

Source: Unpublished study of
Estonian immigration by Tõnu
Parming, University of Maryland.

1938	91	1955	1773
1939	95	1956	1846
		1957	1432
1940	116	1958	739
1941	114	1959	523
1942	162		
1943	198	1960	414
1944	261	1961	422
		1962	362
1945	138	1963	241
1946	105	1964	182
1947	107		
1948	63	1965	159
1949	104	1966	127
		1967	95
1950	139	1968	96
1951	101		
1952	162		
1953	175		
1954	335		

The above figures represent people
who have acquired American citizenship whose "former country of al-
legiance was Estonia." Thus, the
figures do not take into account all
Estonians in the United States, some
of whom had acquired citizenship in
a third country before arriving in
the United States.

Table 3

EDUCATIONAL LEVEL OF ESTONIAN-AMERICAN YOUTH: 1968

Source: From a study of Estonian
assimilation in the United States
by Tõnu Parming, published in the
Estonian-language cultural journal _Mana_, Volume 13, No. 1, 1970.

	22-years old or younger in 1968	23-years old or older in 1968
has not completed high school	1.5%	0.7%
high school graduate, but no college	15.0%	11.3%
some college, but no degree	69.0%	24.2%
bachelor's degree, but no graduate school	13.0%	33.4%
master's degree or working on it	1.5%	21.2%
doctoral degree or working on it	---	9.2%
TOTALS	100.0% (68)	100.0% (293)

The study was based on youth confirmed at the two
Estonian Lutheran congregations in New York City
between 1953 and 1965. Confirmation in the church
usually takes place in the late teens. The figures
in the table are for both sexes together. Of the
youth who were 23-years old or older and were male,
26.4% had or were working on master's degrees and
12.6% had or were working on doctoral degrees.

Table 4

NUMBER OF FIRST AND SECOND GENERATION ESTONIANS
IN AMERICA: 1950, 1960, 1970

Source: Unpublished study of
Estonian immigration by Tõnu
Parming, University of Maryland.

state	1950	1960	1970
Alabama	25	5	14
Alaska	unk	33	66
Arizona	5	53	77
Arkansas	15	4	22
California	895	2572	2871
Colorado	20	81	272
Connecticut	340	1000	825
Delaware	25	106	153
District of Columbia	60	91	64
Florida	185	554	656
Georgia	35	79	119
Hawaii	unk	11	12
Idaho	15	16	39
Illinois	510	1437	1449
Indiana	90	180	178
Iowa	155	131	108
Kansas	25	23	31
Kentucky	25	13	45
Louisiana	15	81	70
Maine	20	17	17
Maryland	245	515	884
Massachusetts	330	402	688
Michigan	330	637	632
Minnesota	170	430	381
Mississippi	60	0	23
Missouri	40	76	75
Montana	25	65	44
Nebraska	50	71	71
Nevada	10	11	0
New Hampshire	20	34	27

Table 4, continued

state	1950	1960	1970
New Jersey	1010	2071	2090
New Mexico	30	32	42
New York	3575	6002	5109
North Carolina	75	59	55
North Dakota	80	44	112
Ohio	220	674	528
Oklahoma	35	48	32
Oregon	160	310	562
Pennsylvania	320	486	605
Rhode Island	10	76	49
South Carolina	25	56	40
South Dakota	40	32	24
Tennessee	45	37	13
Texas	140	262	201
Utah	5	4	33
Vermont	15	24	85
Virginia	110	141	197
Washington	260	490	523
West Virginia	15	3	16
Wisconsin	145	338	278
Wyoming	30	21	0
TOTALS	10,085	19,938	20,507

These figures show the number of people who
were born in Estonia (first generation) or
who had at least one parent born in Estonia
but were themselves born in the United States
(second generation). Excluded are Estonians
born in other countries and their children.

Table   5

ESTONIAN COMMUNITY CENTERS IN AMERICA, 1975

Baltimore Estonian House
1932 Belair Road
Baltimore, Maryland
21213

Chicago Estonian House
PO Box 95
Prairie View, Illinois
60069

Lakewood Estonian House
Cross Street/New Egypt Rd.
Jackson, New Jersey
[mail: PO Box 616
Lakewood, New Jersey 08701]

Los Angeles Estonian House
1306 West 24th Street
Los Angeles, California
90007

Miami Estonian House
111 West 29th Street
Hialeah, Florida
33012

Minneapolis Estonian House
1417-19 East Lake Street
Minneapolis, Minnesota
55407

New York Estonian House
243 East 34th Street
New York City, New York
10016

Seabrook Estonian House
Seabrook, New Jersey
08302

San Francisco Estonian
   House
[in process of purchase]

Table 6

REGISTER OF MAJOR ESTONIAN-AMERICAN ORGANIZATIONS:
1975

Organizations of International Scope

Committee for a Free Estonia (New York City)
Estonian World Council (New York City)
League of Estonian Chess Clubs Abroad (New York City)
World Association of Estonians, Inc. (New York City)
World Legion of Estonian Liberation (Andover, Connecticut)
World Society of Estonian Literature (New York City)

Organizations of National Scope

Archives of Estonian Aviation (Torrance, California)
Association of Estonian Agronomists in the United
    States (Amherst, Massachusetts)
Association of Estonian Girl Guide Leaders in the United
    States (Schenectady, New York)
Association of Estonian Journalists in the United States
    (New York City)
Association of Estonian Teachers in the United States
    (New York City)

Central Council of Estonian Military Officers (New York
    City)
Council of Estonian Boy Scouts in the United States
    (New York City)
Council of Estonian Girl Guides in the United States
    (New York City)
Council of Estonian Scoutmasters in the United States
    (Lakewood, New Jersey)

Estonian Aid, Inc. (New York City)
Estonian American Citizens Association (New York City)
Estonian American National Council (New York City)
Estonian American Republican National Committee (New
    York City)
Estonian Archives in the United States (Lakewood, New
    Jersey)
Estonian Athletic Union in the United States, Inc.
    (Lakewood, New Jersey)
Estonian Evangelical Lutheran First Synod (New York City)
Estonian Evangelical Lutheran Synod of Chicago (New York
    City)
Estonian Film Center (New York City)
Estonian Learned Society in America (New York City)

Estonian Music Center (New York City)
Estonian P.E.N. Club (Farmington, Connecticut)
Estonian Relief Committee, Inc. (New York City)
Estonian Salute to Bicentennial '76, Inc. (Baltimore)
Estonian School Fund in the United States, Inc. (New
    York City)
Estonian Schools Center (Willimantic, Connecticut)
Estonian Scientific and Technical Conferences (Philadel-
    phia)
Estonian Students Association (New York City)
Estonian Students Association Alumni Council (New York
    City)
Estonian Students Fund in the United States, Inc. (New
    York City)

Federation of Associations for the Advancement of Esto-
    nian Youth, Inc. (Lakewood, New Jersey)
Foundation for Estonian Arts and Letters, Inc. (New
    York City)
Henrik Visnapuu Memorial Literary Fund (New York City)
League of Estonian Academic Fraternities in the United
    States (New York City)
League of Estonian Women's Clubs (New York City)
Legion of Estonian Liberation, Inc. (New York City)
Ludwig Juht Memorial Estonian Music Fund (New York City)

Regional Organizations

Estonian League of the West Coast
Estonian League of the West Coast, Council of Past Pre-
    sidents
Midwest Estonian Youth Association
West Coast Alliance Mission

Local Organizations

CALIFORNIA

Estonian Society of Fresno

Estonian Society of Los Angeles, Inc.
Estonian Evangelical Lutheran Congregation - Los Angeles
Los Angeles Estonian Supplementary School
Los Angeles Estonian Boy Scout Troop Tulehoidja
Los Angeles Estonian Girl Guide Troop Taaratütred
Los Angeles Association of Estonian War Veterans
Los Angeles Estonian Republican Club
Los Angeles Estonian Women's Club
Los Angeles Estonian Mixed Chorus
Los Angeles Estonian Orthodox Congregation
Los Angeles Estonian Pentecostal Congregation

Estonian Society of San Francisco
Estonian Evangelical Lutheran Congregation - San Francisco
San Francisco Estonian Supplementary School
San Francisco Estonian Boy Scout Troop
San Francisco Association of Estonian War Veterans
San Francisco Estonian Mixed Chorus
San Francisco Estonian Orthodox Congregation

CONNECTICUT

Connecticut Estonian Society, Inc.
Estonian Evangelical Lutheran Congregation - Connecticut
Connecticut Estonian Supplementary School
Connecticut Association for the Advancement of Estonian Youth
Connecticut Estonian Boy Scout Troop Vikerlased
Connecticut Estonian Girl Guide Troop Põhjatütred
Connecticut Association of Estonian War Veterans
Connecticut Estonian Republican Club

Danielson Estonian Women's Club

DELAWARE

Delaware Valley Estonian Boy Scout Troop Pohjataht
Wilmington Estonian Supplementary School

DISTRICT OF COLUMBIA

Estonian Society of Washington
Washington Estonian Supplementary School
Washington Association for the Advancement of Estonian Youth
Washington Estonian Boy Scout Troop
Washington Association of Estonian War Veterans
Washington Estonian Youth Club

FLORIDA

Estonian-American Cultural Club of Miami

ILLINOIS

Assembly of Estonian Organizations in Illinois

Chicago Estonian Society, Inc.
Estonian Evangelical Lutheran Congregation of St. Paul - Chicago
Estonian Evangelical Lutheran First Congregation - Chicago
Estonian Evangelical Lutheran First Reformed Congregation - Chicago

Chicago Estonian Supplementary School
Chicago Estonian Boy Scout Troop Pōhjapojad
Chicago Estonian Aid Committee
Chicago Estonian Folk Dance Group Mustjala
Chicago Estonian Mixed Chorus
Chicago Estonian Theatre
Chicago Estonian Orthodox Congregation

Estonian Association of Northern Illinois, Inc.
Northern Illinois Estonian Girl Guide Troop Tammela
    tütred
Northern Illinois Estonian Mixed Chorus

INDIANA

Estonian Society of Indianapolis
Estonian Evangelical Lutheran Congregation of St. Paul -
    Indianapolis

MARYLAND

Baltimore Estonian Society, Inc.
Estonian Evangelical Lutheran Congregation --Baltimore/
    Washington
Estonian Evangelical Lutheran Congregation of St. Mark -
    Baltimore/Washington
Baltimore Estonian Supplementary School
Baltimore Association for the Advancement of Estonian
    Youth
Baltimore Estonian Boy Scout Troop Pōhjakotkad
Baltimore Estonian Girl Guide Troop Tormitütred
Baltimore Estonian Female Chorus
Baltimore Estonian Folk Dance Group
Baltimore Estonian Male Chorus
Baltimore Estonian Modern Rhythmic Dance Group
Baltimore Estonian Mutual Aid Burial Society

Estonian American Republican Club of Maryland
Jüri Mandre Music Fund, Inc.
Maryland Association of Estonian War Veterans

MASSACHUSETTS

Boston Estonian Society, Inc.

MICHIGAN

Detroit Estonian Society Kodu
Estonian Evangelical Lutheran Congregation - Detroit
Detroit Association of Estonian War Veterans
Estonian American Republican Club of Michigan

MINNESOTA

Estonian Society of Duluth

St. Paul Estonian Religious Group

Estonian Association of Minnesota (Minneapolis)
Estonian Evangelical Lutheran Congregation - Minneapolis
Minnesota Estonian Supplementary School (Minneapolis)
Minnesota Estonian Chess Club (Minneapolis)
Minnesota Estonian Folkcrafts Club (Minnesota)
Minnesota Estonian Mixed Chorus (Minneapolis)
Minnesota Estonian Orchestra (Minneapolis)
Minnesota Estonian Theatre (Minneapolis)
Minnesota Estonian Women's Club (Minneapolis)
Minnesota Estonian Youth Group (Minneapolis)
Minnesota Estonian Bridge Club (Minneapolis)

NEW JERSEY

Estonian Evangelical Lutheran Congregation - Bergen
    County
Estonian Evangelical Lutheran Congregation - Paterson
Northern New Jersey Estonian Girl Guide Troop Linda-
    tütred

Lakewood Estonian Association, Inc.
Estonian Evangelical Lutheran Congregation of the Holy
    Ghost - Lakewood (sub-parish at Red Bank)
Lakewood Estonian Supplementary School
Lakewood Association for the Advancement of Estonian
    Youth
Lakewood Estonian Boy Scout Troops Lembitu
Lakewood Estonian Girl Guide Troop Kungla
Lakewood Association of Estonian War Veterans
Lakewood Estonian Athletic Club
Lakewood Estonian Bridge and Chess Club
Lakewood Estonian Folkdance Group
Lakewood Estonian Mixed Chorus
Lakewood Estonian Philatelic Club
Lakewood Estonian Rifle Club
Lakewood Estonian Theatre
Lakewood Estonian Women's Club
Lakewood Estonian Women's Folkcrafts Club

Estonian American Republican Club of Central New Jersey

Estonian Association at Seabrook
Estonian Evangelical Lutheran Congregation - Seabrook
Seabrook Association of Estonian War Veterans

NEW YORK

Estonian Association of Albany and Schenectady, Inc.
Albany and Schenectady Estonian Supplementary School
Schenectady Estonian Girl Guide Troop Tähetütred

Estonian Society of Buffalo
Estonian Evangelical Lutheran Congregation of St. Paul -
    Buffalo
Buffalo Estonian Supplementary School
Buffalo Estonian Boy Scout Troop Toompea kaitsjad
Buffalo Estonian Girl Guide Troop Põhjatäht
Buffalo Estonian Mixed Chorus
Western New York Association of Estonian War Veterans

Estonian Society of Long Island
Long Island Estonian Supplementary School
Long Island Estonian Boy Scout Troop
Long Island Estonian Girl Guide Troop Virmalised
Long Island Association of Estonian War Veterans
Long Island Estonian Folk Dance Group
Long Island Estonian Theatre
Long Island Estonian Women's Club
Long Island Estonian Youth Orchestra

Mid-Hudson Estonian Association, Inc.
Poughkeepsie Association of Estonian War Veterans

New York Estonian Educational Society, Inc.
Estonian Evangelical Lutheran Congregation of Lexington
    Avenue
Estonian Evangelical Lutheran Congregation of St. Paul
    (sub-parishes at Albany/Schenectady and Syracuse)
New York Estonian Supplementary School
New York Association for the Advancement of Estonian
    Youth
New York Estonian Boy Scout Troops Viiking
New York Estonian Girl Guide Troops Linnutee
New York Association of Estonian War Veterans
New York Estonian Athletic Club
New York Estonian Bridge Club
New York Estonian Chess Club
New York Estonian Children's Camp Booster Committee
New York Estonian Female Chorus
New York Estonian Folk Dance Group Saare vikat
New York Estonian Male Chorus
New York Estonian Modern Rhythmic Dance Group
New York Estonian Philatelic Society
New York Estonian Supplementary School Parent-Teachers
    Association
New York Estonian Theatre
New York Estonian Women's Club

New York Estonian Youth Club
Council of Friends of the New York Estonian Children's
   Camp

New York City Estonian Baptist Congregation
New York City Estonian Orthodox Congregation
New York Estonian Pentecostal Congregation
New York Estonian Seventh Day Adventists Congregation

OHIO

Estonian Association of Cleveland, Inc.
Estonian Evangelical Lutheran Congregation - Cleveland
Cleveland-Columbus Estonian Folk Dance Group Targajala

Estonian Society of Columbus
Ohio Association of Estonian War Veterans

OREGON

Estonian Society in Portland
Estonian Evangelical Lutheran Congregation - Portland
Portland Estonian Supplementary School
Portland Association of Estonian War Veterans

PENNSYLVANIA

Estonian Evangelical Lutheran Congregation - Philadelphia
Philadelphia Estonian Mixed Chorus

WISCONSIN

Estonian Society of Milwaukee

WASHINGTON

Estonian Society of Seattle
Estonian Evangelical Lutheran Congregation - Seattle
Seattle Estonian Supplementary School
Seattle Association of Estonian War Veterans

BIBLIOGRAPHICAL AIDS

There are essentially only two known published English-language sources on the Estonians in America, both by Joseph Slabey Roucek. His article, "The American Estonians," appeared first in the periodical Baltic Countries, Volume 2, September 1936 (published in Torun, Poland). A revised version was published as a chapter in the book One America (Prentice-Hall, 1952), which Roucek coedited with Francis J. Brown. Both articles are general and brief, and neither carries the story beyond World War Two.

The materials in the present work have been almost totally based on Estonian-language sources and documents found in the archives of Estonian-American organizations. A substantial part of the information came from the following periodicals: Eesti Amerika Postimees (The Estonian American Courier), a monthly newspaper published in New York City and Boston from March, 1897, to July, 1911; Meie Tee (Our Path), a monthly magazine published in New York City from 1931 to the present; and Vaba Eesti Sõna (The Free Estonian Word), a weekly newspaper published in New York City from 1949 to the present. Also of considerable value were sources such as Väliseestlase kalender (The Calendar for the Estonian Abroad), published annually from 1953 to the present in New York City by Nordic Press under the editorship of Erich Ernits; and Välis-Eesti almanak (The Estonia Abroad Almanac), published monthly in Tallinn, Estonia, from 1929 to 1940 [after the first few years the periodical was published under the abbreviated title of Välis Eesti]. Other useful sources included Eugenie Mutt's "Ameerika eestlased" (The Estonians of America), in the Estonian periodical Eesti Hõim (The Estonian Tribe), Number 4, 1928; Välis Eesti tegelased (Estonian Activists Abroad), published in Tallinn, Estonia, by the Välis Eesti Ühing (Estonia Abroad Association) in 1939; and Uue-Ilma Juubeli Album 1909-1934 (The Jubilee Album of the New World), published in New York City by the Estonian-language newspaper Uus Ilm (The New World).

Many of these source materials are available only in the archives and libraries of various Estonian-American organizations, and some, such as issues of the Estonian socialist and later communist newspaper Uus Ilm, are available only in private collections. Estonian-American organizations which have especially valuable collections are:

The Estonian Archives in
  the United States
607 East 7th Street
Lakewood, New Jersey
        08701

The New York Estonian
  Educational Society
Estonian House
243 East 34th Street
New York, New York 10016

Another valuable source of information would be:

    The Consulate General of the
       Republic of Estonia
    9 Rockefeller Plaza
    New York, New York 10020

Interested persons might, additionally, contact their local Estonian-American organizations, which are listed in Table 6 in the appendix of the present work. Addresses of Estonian Community Centers in the country are given in Table 5. Another centralized information source would be the Estonian American National Council in New York City (Estonian House address given above).

Lastly, the Estonian Learned Society in America published in 1974 a general <u>Bibliography</u> <u>of</u> English-<u>Language</u> <u>Sources</u> on <u>Estonia</u>, containing nearly 700 entries. Copies may be ordered from the society (Estonian House address given above).

NAME INDEX